Fulltiming

An Introduction to Full-Time RVing

Gaylord Maxwell

First printing: May, 1991
Second printing: May, 1992
Third printing: July, 1994 (Revised)

Produced at North Country Publishing by Mary Shierman, Melissa Rockwood, Alison Mitchell and Opal Gerwig, under the direction of Ivar Nelson and Patricia Hart.

Cover design by Melissa Rockwood.

Cover photograph taken near Durango, CO by Robert Longsdorf, Jr.

Additional copies may be obtained from Gaylord Maxwell, 3601 Calle Tecate, Camarillo, CA 93012. Please send $9.95 + $1.50 shipping.

This book is dedicated to Margie,
my wife, my companion, my friend,
and my sweetheart for over four decades.

Acknowledgments

Although the information in *An Introduction to Full-time RVing* draws upon our thirty-plus years of experience as RVers, I must give credit to the original source for nearly every bit of knowledge I claim: our fellow RVers. Like a sponge, I soak up every "how-to" lecture, every "where-to" recommendation, every yarn, and file that information away for recall when I need it. Much recollecting was done to fill the pages that follow. Thank you, RV friends.

I would also like to express gratitude to my friends at TL Enterprises — especially Bill Estes and Mike Schneider — whose encouragement has been much appreciated. My very special thanks go to Maxye Henry, whose ever-cheerful voice on the telephone is my happy link to the "hub of power," and whose conscientious attention to the mundane chores that keep us functioning relatively smoothly out on the "front lines" is appreciated much more than she knows. And I'm very grateful to Rena Copperman, who took many hours of her own time to do the editing.

Both Margie and I would like to express our heartfelt gratitude to Rick Rouse, president of TL Enterprises, Inc., who, almost five years ago, gave us the job of representing his company while we roam *the greatest vacation country in the world via the greatest way of doing it.* Thanks, Rick, for giving us the best job in the world!

Preface

Before I read any book, especially those written by "authorities on the subject," I like to know something about those authorities. I want evidence that they are truly qualified to give advice about whatever the subject may be.

I assume that most of you who are reading these words would also appreciate some assurance that my credentials are sufficient to put me in a position to "advise." So, in the hope that I may convince you to continue beyond this page because I might know something worth finding out, here is my background:

My first serious career was as a teacher, but after seventeen years of trying, with varying degrees of success, to make U.S. History exciting for high schoolers, I opted for a new vocation. An interest in camping and RVing led me into that field, and, for the next two decades, I did my best to encourage and teach people to camp and travel while I earned a living selling them recreational vehicles.

Apparently I succumbed to my own sales pitch because over a dozen years ago, Margie (my "bride" of forty-five years) and I sold the business and embraced a lifestyle that called for most of our time to be spent RVing—a lifestyle that fit perfectly with my former secondary, now primary, occupation as a writer for *MotorHome* and *Trailer Life* magazines.

In addition to my writing duties, Margie and I have served as Industry Relations Directors for TL Enterprises for the past eight years. Duties in these roles consist generally of doing things to make RVing better for RVers. In addition, I also give seminars and make consumer-care-oriented speeches at RV industry conventions. For four years, I have served as chairman of the Consumer Care Commission, established by the Recreational Vehicle Dealer Association (RVDA), which brings together representatives of the various segments of the RV industry to study consumer-related problems in the industry and to recommend remedies.

As with many RVers, we started camping in tents when we were young. Our first experience with RVs (they weren't even called RVs back then) was with a tent trailer. For most of our outings during the years our kids were growing up, we used various sizes and styles of Apaches (which we also sold). Then came the truck-and-camper phase—even a *big* 10 footer! A succession of travel trailers and even a fifth-wheel or two preceded our shift to motorhomes nearly two decades ago. Since that time, we've owned ten motorhomes—and we're shopping for a new one now!

We've traveled in all forty-eight of the lower states, most of which we've been in many times, and all of which we expect to visit many more times. I have a United States map on which I mark roads we've traveled, and pretty soon it will be solid black! (Most years, we cover a minimum of 20,000 miles.)

Although I haven't kept a record, I daresay we've put at least a half-million miles on assorted RVs. We've camped in, traveled in, visited in, lived in, and worked in various sizes and styles for over three decades, enjoying (occasionally suffering) every type of RV destination available, from boondocking in the desert to elegant resorts. We've camped alone and we've rallied with 10,000 other RVers. In short, if we've missed anything, I don't know what it was—but I'll keep looking for it.

Although we are not fulltimers, we spend more than eight months each year in a motorhome, but we "vacation" during the summer at our place in Idaho's panhandle, where we spend much of our time entertaining visiting RV friends. To address the question of how we can be so-called authorities on fulltiming when we actually aren't practitioners ourselves, I simply respond, Does a bartender have to be a drunk to make a good cocktail? The fact is that I have spent many years informing myself on the subject as much as by learning from others as from our own experiences. Consequently, what follows is actually a view of fulltiming very much influenced by what we have *seen* and *heard* combined with what we have *felt* and *done.* We hope these views will be useful to readers, especially those who are considering fulltiming and who have many questions about life on the road.

This book is directed at experienced RVers who are trying to make up their minds whether or not to hit the road full time, as well as those who are completely uninitiated (but dreaming). It generally doesn't answer questions directly as much as it offers information and options to assist readers in making their own decisions. The various personal experiences I relate or refer to are provided, not to instruct the reader to do things my way, but to give reference points for self-direction. That approach is used because of my personal wariness and reluctance to pay much heed to people who try to tell me how I should do things. In my judgment, what these people do is to tell me what *they* prefer, the way *they* do things, and that might not be what I or someone else should do at all. I prefer to have options from which I may choose and modify to suit my particular needs and likes.

The reality is that there is no more a single way of RV fulltiming than there is only one way of living a regular life in a house anywhere. A common factor is that RV fulltimers are on wheels, but the variations from that point on are as diverse as people anywhere. Wise people will inform themselves as much as possible about the many options available, do some experimenting and investigating, and choose a path suited to them. RV fulltiming is very democratic; you can have it *your* way because what you make of it is largely up to you.

Good luck! I hope we meet down the road.

Contents

Introduction

A secret — sometimes not so secret — desire of many Americans is to move into a trailer or motorhome and just roam around the country, staying where they wish as long as they wish, seeing all the wonderful scenery, enjoying the natural beauty of our country, fishing, filming, painting, or doing whatever their "thing" is without concern for schedules or clocks or what other people want — in short, a desire to be *free*.

Perhaps it's the heritage passed on to us by Daniel Boone, Kit Carson, the forty-niners, and the countless scores of our restless ancestors. Included are the Joe Smiths and Bill Joneses who didn't achieve anything noble or great but, like those who did famous deeds, couldn't hack the restrictions imposed by living in one place. They knew there were roads to be taken, bends in the river to follow, mountains to climb, deserts to cross, sights to be seen, and riches to be gained. Like an itch, the yearning to go places and see things has to be scratched, and the only way to do that is to *go*. For the fulltimer, the itch is permanent and requires continuous "scratching."

Thousands of today's Americans do just that. Estimates are that more than three quarters of a million people now live full time in their RVs. My personal opinion is that this estimate is too conservative. Unfortunately, since counting "birds on the wing" is difficult, we have no precise number. Suffice it to say that there are lots of fulltimers, and the number is growing. In fact, if only half the people who talk about it actually take up the lifestyle, we'll need a lot of new facilities to accommodate them in the years to come.

Perhaps before we get too involved with the subject of fulltiming, we ought to determine just what we include in the term. Strictly defined, the words *full time* mean living 365 days a year in an RV. Like pregnancy, there can't be an "almost." One is either pregnant or not pregnant; similarly, one is either a fulltimer or not. Many RVers fall into a category that I call *extended timers* — those who spend a great deal of time (like six months a year) on the road. Most of them still have homes somewhere, where they live for some time each year. They still have roots, a fact that differentiates them from the true fulltimer.

However, since many of the needs, experiences, joys, and rewards of extended timing are similar to those of fulltiming, much of what I have to say is pertinent to both. Indeed, the extended-timing period is often the *schooling* period for fulltiming. RVers "test the waters" for six- to eight-month periods and learn the lessons that will guide them in their preparations for fulltiming and in their later travels.

So, for my purposes in *An Introduction to Full-time RVing*, the information is directed toward those who are interested in extended timing, as well as those who are preparing for the whole nine yards.

Chapter 1
What Are Fulltimers Like?

One of the first questions that people who are considering fulltiming ask is: Am I the kind of person who would fit the lifestyle? That question leads to another: What kind of people are fulltimers?

It would be difficult to construct a perfect model of a typical fulltimer, but there are some basic personality characteristics that seem to be common. Persons unsure of whether or not their psyches match those of the model should feel quite confident of success if they do indeed fit a general profile.

Qualities of a Fulltimer

There are at least seven characteristics of a successful fulltimer: dissatisfaction, curiosity, a sense of adventure, gregariousness, daring, patience, and compatibility.

Dissatisfaction

If a person is completely satisfied with the type of life he or she is living, then there's probably no reason to change to something different and risk the unknown. Most people who consider drastic changes in the way they live or do things aren't totally happy with the way they are presently living. They may not be exactly unhappy, but they are looking for something new or different; they want change. In short, they are dissatisfied with life the way it is. So they look to something else, something more attractive, more exciting, to give them more satisfaction in their lives.

People contemplating full-time RVing usually fit in the dissatisfied category. However, it should be pointed out that sometimes would-be fulltimers' perceptions of the lifestyle are over-glamorized and over-simplified. The consequence can be that the reality doesn't match the ideal, and disillusionment results. Just as with most endeavors, attitudes and expectations must reasonably coincide with the realities if success is to be achieved. Fulltiming has some negative aspects — make no mistake about that. People who can't adjust to or accept these negatives will probably find that fulltiming, rather than being a dream come true, is a nightmare.

Curiosity

In most cases, show me a fulltimer and I'll show you a person who has multi-interests — someone who likes to explore, to see, to do new things. Fulltimers usually like to tour old houses, browse at gun shows, dally at flea markets. New RVs and their accompanying gadgets fascinate these people. Poring over maps and planning new trips are favorite pastimes. Stories other people tell about "fabulous places" they've been to tempt them and set them to itching. Usually they are deeply involved with the world around them.

A Sense of Adventure

Like their footloose-and-fancy-free predecessors, the pioneers that opened America up, fulltimers want to find out what is around the bend, what is over the hill, what is down the road. They want to see and experience new things. They think a good reason to take a road is simply the fact that they've never been on it before.

Gregariousness

Most fulltimers are people oriented; they mix with neighbors in campgrounds and parks or wherever they are. Formal introductions aren't necessary for neighborly chatting. Unlike city people who cast their eyes downward when they meet other folks on sidewalks, they look other people in the eye and say, "Howdy." Parties, especially the impromptu kind, are a crucial part of their social life. Often these parties are simply a few couples bringing their chairs and perhaps refreshments to gather under someone's awning for chit-chat and story swapping. (A problem in getting this book done is that I keep riding my bicycle around the RV park we're in and stopping regularly to shoot the bull with other RVers.)

Many fulltimers find their circle of friends grows more and more to include other RVers. Visiting takes place in RV parks, campgrounds, or at club rallies. Most social interaction is spontaneous and informal.

Daring

It takes more than a little nerve to be a full-time RVer. In the first place, just attempting it requires considerable spirit. To tackle mountain roads, city traffic, and other challenging conditions on our highways at the wheel of a monstrous multi-ton rig is not a job for wimps. Simply because fulltiming often involves heading into the unknown, practitioners need be more than a little blessed with courage.

Patience

Impatience simply doesn't square with the RV lifestyle, which is basically a "take-it-easy" mode. Anyone who has driven his or her rig up I-70 between Grand Junction, Colorado, and Denver or White Bird grade on U.S. 95 south of Lewiston, Idaho, knows how important it is to be able to play it cool when thundering along wide-open at seventeen miles per hour for miles and miles!

A reality of this lifestyle is that RVers live very close to each other in parks and share many common facilities, so patience (and tolerance) is a necessary virtue. When the snoring you hear at midnight is coming through your open bedroom window via your neighbor's open bedroom window, the admonition to love your fellow man and woman can become a serious challenge.

Compatibility

Quite simply, there isn't much fighting room in an RV, so traveling companions must *like* (nothing to do with *love* or *passion*) each other. Full-time couples are together twenty-four hours a day—always within shouting, often within striking, distance! So, if they don't really like each other, the odds of enjoying fulltiming are remote. Of course, getting a larger RV is a partial solution — there's more fighting room in a 30 footer than in a 20 footer. (After thirty years of RVing, Margie and I are now up to 40 feet.)

Of course, one could list other characteristics that describe fulltimers, but these are the main ones. One doesn't necessarily have to fit a mold that includes all of them, but I think it would be difficult to be a fulltimer and not have any of them.

Who Doesn't Fit?

Who definitely does not fit the full-timer mold? Actually, there are all kinds of people successfully, or relatively successfully, fulltiming, even some old grouches whom I suspect have taken up life on the road simply because they can't get along with neighbors at a fixed place. Of course, they don't get along with other RVers either, but they're easy to move away from. The kind of people who definitely don't fit as fulltimers are the "old poops," that is, people who don't do anything, don't think anything, and don't want to deviate from what is to them a comfortable state of lethargy. An old poop generally likes to tilt back in a lounge chair with a beer and chips and watch anything (including commercials and old movies) on television.

Chapter 2
What Must You Give Up to Be a Fulltimer?

There are several items one must be willing to forego to follow the full-timing lifestyle. They include:

A Fixed Place

Most people are associated with a *fixed place*, that is, they have an address where anyone who cares to investigate can find them. Whether it is a street number, rural route box, or an apartment number, it is a definite place, and the mail carrier, the UPS delivery person, the police officer, or any person in the world who can read a map will be able to locate you or send something to you. The fact that most people refer to where they live as "my place" is a clue as to how people feel about their own space on this planet.

When you take up fulltiming, you generally give up that fixed place, and people no longer associate you with a geographical spot. It even confuses the kids. For example, we call our three children every weekend, and the first question they ask is usually, "Where are you?" We are no longer identified with a fixed place. We do have an address to receive mail and a phone number where we can be called (see pages 23–25), but neither is where we actually are. Nearly all fulltimers I've met say they're happy not to have a "place." In fact, they feel that their rig is home, and they are content to be wherever it happens to be parked.

The Familiar

Another element one gives up for fulltiming is the *familiar:*

people, places, and things. In a house, one becomes accustomed to furniture, equipment, fixtures, doors, and windows in exactly the same place every day, year in and year out. You see the same people regularly—the mail carrier, the grocer, the people you work with, relatives, friends, club members, and others. When you walk out your door, the same steps, the same trees and shrubs, the same driveway, the same street greet you. All that is gone when you take to the road full time. We find it interesting to awaken in the morning and wonder where we are. Of course, the motorhome is familiar, but outside, all may be quite strange. That's the beauty of it all—something new and different to start the day.

Routine

We're all accustomed to routines in our daily lives. We get up and follow exactly the same steps every morning, and more of them through the day: the same breakfast at the same place at the table, the same route to work, the same job, and the same people. All that changes when you take up fulltiming. Admittedly, you get into some other routines, but you do a lot of things differently because you're in new surroundings and have more opportunities to go in various directions.

Chores

You give up a lot of old chores when you become a fulltimer: no more house to paint, no more lawns to mow, no shrubs to trim, no driveway to sweep, no big house to vacuum and dust, no garage to tidy up. As might be expected, you pick up a few new chores—keeping the rig spiffed up or fixing the gadgets that break. But the housekeeping and maintenance work in keeping up a trailer or motorhome is infinitely less than in maintaining a home and lot.

Expenses

And you give up some expenses, as well—property taxes,

utility bills, and house maintenance costs among them. Of course, you pick up some expenses you didn't have before—campground fees, higher gasoline bills, and some maintenance expenses. However, fulltiming can easily be *much* less expensive than living in a regular home (see also pages 48–53).

Chapter 3
What You Get
from Fulltiming

Giving up certain comforts to travel full time also means gaining some new aspects to your life, including the following.

A New Freedom

Fulltimers agree that the main advantage they gain from the fulltiming lifestyle is *freedom* — freedom from the restrictions and obligations that a normal life in a home impose: freedom from routine, freedom from the myriad chores of maintaining a property, and freedom from boredom. You get the opportunity to choose where you'll be, when you'll be there, and what you will do when you get there. You'll have a few new chores, of course, but you'll have plenty of time to do them and still enjoy special places you travel to.

An RV can be as plush and comfortable as you wish (or can afford), with many of the amenities of a regular home. Television, stereo, comfortable chairs and sofas, a compact but complete kitchen (with microwave oven, blender, built-in coffeemaker, etc.), functional bathroom, comfortable queen bed, excellent heating and cooling systems, and generally adequate storage are common features on today's rigs. Some even have washer/dryers, trash compactors, dishwashers, satellite TV, and heaven knows what's next. In short, many of the normal functions and aspects of everyday living stay relatively the same in an RV. One does not — repeat — *does not* have to give up comfort to become a full-time RVer. It is only a slight exaggeration, perhaps, to paraphrase Patrick Henry thus: To become a fulltimer means only to lose the chains that bind you to convention.

Opportunities

I'm constantly amazed at the *new* opportunities that crop up for fulltimers: Opportunities to do, see, and be a part of the world that never became available in "regular" life. For example, many RV parks, particularly those that cater to snowbirds, offer activities that include such activities as arts and crafts, dancing, sports and physical exercises, and cultural offerings. We have two friends who took painting classes (which they had never been exposed to before) several years ago. Both took to art and have since become quite proficient at it. In fact, one of our friends now sells her paintings for as much as $100 each. Had it not been for the class offering in the park in which they were staying, they probably never would have had the opportunity to develop their talents.

Other friends have taken up square dancing and have already progressed through the various stages until they are now quite expert. They were in their mid-sixties when they had their first lesson at the RV park where they were wintering. Many RVers, particularly fulltimers, find new interests, in part because they have the time to pursue them. Exposure to these opportunities came about simply because they pursued their dreams of life on wheels.

Education

To repeat a cliche: Travel is broadening (unfortunately it can be both mentally and physically so). There are no better geography lessons than those learned from travel. Many fulltimers eventually sample the entire United States and know firsthand what the terrain is like, the various climates, how people live, what people do for a living, what crops are grown where, the names of rivers and mountains, and much more. I get a kick out of hearing a group of people who have been fulltiming for a long time discuss places they've been. Conversations are spotted with questions like: Were you ever at?. . . Or, Did you ever see? . . . Frequently the response is, Yeah, we were there in. . . . And so the conversations go on about details that they all are familiar with.

Many fulltimers are fascinated about our history and like to learn stories about the past in the places they visit. History is much more meaningful if you are standing at Kitty Hawk reading the marker designating the spot where the Wright brothers flew, or on the battlefield at Gettysburg peering into the rocks at Devil's Den, where Northern troops fired at charging Southerners, or at the reconstructed fort at Fort Clatsop, where Lewis and Clark spent a miserable winter in Oregon. Thousands of such sites lure history buffs, and these visitors generally leave with a better knowledge of our history and a greater appreciation for our country.

Fulltimers have many opportunities to learn about science and culture by visiting museums. For example, our space program makes a lot more sense after one has visited Cape Canaveral, Florida (particularly if they are fortunate enough to witness a launch as we were). Huntsville, Alabama, where most of our rockets were developed, also has a great space museum and provides an excellent, brief history of space exploration and our part in it. The NASA Space Center in Houston rounds out the "big three" for very realistic lessons on our space history.

The Cowboy Hall of Fame in Oklahoma City is devoted to the memory of rodeo riders and our cowboy history. Another great museum that recalls our Western heritage is the Buffalo Bill Cody Museum in Cody, Wyoming. RVers flock to both.

Dinosaur National Monument in Utah is a marvelous working museum and gives a firsthand view of scientists at work uncovering the past. Visitors, many of whom are RVers, come away with a far greater comprehension of the science of paleontology.

I love to tour ships: the *Alabama* at Mobile, the *Texas* at the San Jacinto Monument east of Houston (a double-barreled attraction there), the *Yorktown* at Charleston, the *Constitution* at Boston. Touring these ships, combined with reading all the literature connected with these tours, one almost feels a part of our great wars.

We've been to all of these places and have personally seen both the attractions and the scores of RVs parked in the lots at these attractions. It's obvious to me that we RVers are interested in seeing and knowing.

Also we have a leg up on those who travel by airplanes, cars, buses, or trains because we visit in the comfort of our homes. Often our rig is parked out in the lot of the attraction we're visiting, so we can rest any time, eat any time, or even take a nap in between hitches of touring. That makes for very easy, pleasant learning. Many fulltimers, although lacking in extensive formal education, end up well educated through practical observation and involvement.

New People, Places, and Things

Most people, especially those who are of retirement age, have led rather restricted lives. Until recent years, travel was much more limited than it is now. People stayed close to home most of the time and normally took a vacation once a year, during which time they might have taken a long trip. Generally, their firsthand knowledge of other places was quite limited.

That can change drastically when you go fulltiming. You meet people with diverse backgrounds; you see places you've never seen before; and you find yourself doing things you've never done before. Your circle expands; life can become more interesting.

Excitement

I can't think of anything worse than going through life with nothing but dull routine, day in and day out. To me, the idea of sitting in a rocking chair on a porch all day and jawing with cronies or watching television for six or eight hours every evening is a boring way to live. I like to wake up with the prospect of going somewhere new or doing something exciting every day. I can't picture myself in a life without something to look forward to each day. Fulltimers have every opportunity to do that. All they have to do is select exciting places to visit and go there.

Security

Crime is rampant in America, and it is getting worse. Not since frontier days has personal safety and protection of property been of such great concern. Just read the newspapers, watch television, or listen to the radio and you'll almost be convinced that we live in a war zone. Many people in cities live behind locked, bolted doors and never go out alone or at night. They must constantly be alert for purse snatchers or muggers. They never know when they leave their homes if their belongings will be there when they return. When we lived in Los Angeles County (we left in the late 1970s), Margie always kept our doors locked, even in the daytime, since robberies and rapes during the day were not uncommon. And we lived in a supposedly quiet, safe, college community! Imagine what it is like to be a resident in one labeled "unsafe."

We've all seen investigative news programs showing how many older people in cities live in fear; some even suffer malnutrition because they are afraid to walk on streets in their own neighborhoods to go shopping.

The RV lifestyle is probably the most crime-free way to live. Quite simply, robbers, muggers, rapists, and murderers usually don't travel in trailers and motorhomes. They generally aren't in RV parks and campgrounds. Many RVers think nothing of leaving their rigs with the door open, walking at night alone in parks, or carrying their purses loosely. In most parks, there's a fence between the inhabitants inside and the general population outside. Some parks have guarded entry gates. In short, RVers live without having to fear their fellow man.

Chapter 4
Choosing a Home Base

One of the interesting paradoxes of fulltiming is that you can give up your job, your home, your friends and neighbors, your address, your "place," but you can't give up your *state*. You must claim a state for purposes of licensing — driver's and rig. And if you wish to vote, you have to be a resident somewhere.

Choosing the Right State

To claim a state, you are legally bound to conform with that state's requirements for residence, which in most cases means claiming a specific address as your domicile. In no case does a state *require ownership* of property — just a physical address. A few states allow post-office boxes to meet the address requirement (Delaware, Georgia, Iowa, South Carolina, and, with reservations, a few others).

State Income Tax

Does it make any difference which state one claims for residency? In many cases, the answer is a resounding *yes*. It can make hundreds, even thousands, of dollars of difference every year depending on your particular circumstances. Which states are best for you depend on the money you make and how you spend it. The key word is *taxes*—sales, income, estate, and property. Very simply, in reality, different states have different taxes, and by choosing the right one for your circumstances, you can save a lot of money. For example, if your taxable income is relatively high, you might want to choose a state with no income tax (presently the states of Alaska, Florida, Nevada, South Dakota, Texas, and Washington). You should be aware, however, that state tax laws can change, so you should check the situation with the appropriate agent when you are ready to make the final selection of a state for your home base.

Here's an example of the effect of being a resident of the "right" state: If you pay $4,000 federal tax (and everyone pays federal tax, regardless of the resident state), your state income tax would be $1,000 in Vermont (not necessarily the highest income tax state), but nothing in Texas.

State Sales Tax

If you frequently buy big-ticket items such as new RVs, or generally spend quite a bit of money, you might consider a state with no sales tax (Delaware, Montana, New Hampshire, and Oregon). Again, you should double-check the situation at state-choosing time. An example: If you are a resident of Washington, the sales tax on a new $60,000 motorhome purchased there would be $4,800, but in Oregon there would be no tax. Licenses for RVs range in cost, too. For example, the license for a 40-foot motorhome costing $100,000 purchased in California would be approximately $2,000 for the first year (2 percent of the assessed value of the vehicle), which, added to the sales tax (at 6 percent), means a total tax and license cost of $8,000. In Oregon, the license would cost approximately $150 for **two years**, or a total savings of almost $8,000 the first year and many thousands total for licenses in later years.

Although, in the main, fulltimers don't have huge sums of money to worry about heavy tax liabilities, all have some money, do some spending, and pay some taxes. The point is, all Americans have the right to be residents of any state they choose, and as long as they comply with residence requirement, they are entitled to the rights and privileges of the residents of that state. Since those rights are available, why not exercise them? That's what being an American is all about.

Note: See Appendix II for a complete listing of state laws regarding factors that might influence a home-base selection. However, be aware of the ever-changing nature of tax laws and double-check with the appropriate state agencies before making a final decision.

Chapter 5
Your House: To Sell or Not to Sell?

Whether or not to sell the house can be the stickiest question that prospective fulltimers will face. The answer depends very much on the attitudes of the people involved (usually a couple). If they are convinced that they want to sell, then the answer is obvious. If one or both have doubts that it is what they really want to do, however, then my advice is to hang on to it for a while. Many people have strong emotional attachments to their houses, and, after selling them, they get a bad case of seller's remorse. That can be a very difficult thing to live with — both for the person who is suffering and the one who has to put up with the sufferer.

Selling the House

Of course, if whether or not to go full time depends financially on the sale of the house, then the answer is obvious. In many cases, the funds from the sale of real estate are necessary for acquiring a full-time rig or for living expenses. In fact, the proceeds from the sale of a house are the primary source of income for many fulltimers. In some cases, they sell for cash, invest the money, and receive regular interest or dividend payments. Others prefer to hold mortgages on their houses and receive the higher interest that real-estate contracts earn over what savings accounts pay. That is a route we took many years ago, and today, when CDs are earning only about 7½%, we're still raking in 10% and 11%. Of course, if the pendulum swings the other way and savings' interest rates skyrocket as they did in the early 1980s, long-term mortgages might not look as attractive as they do now.

Keeping the House

RVers who go fulltiming or even extended timing and leave houses behind set themselves up for the opening of the proverbial can of worms. We know. For eleven years, we've left our house for periods of up to eleven months at a time. We've tried every way we know to protect it. Let me tell you, it isn't easy!

Our experiences have ranged all the way from "darn good" to "near disaster." Assaults by flood and fire were the highlights — to say nothing of the cost of keeping the place. We may not be there, but the bills are. Insurance, taxes, phone, power, and the always-necessary maintenance — these things are eternal. But it's a penalty we're willing to pay to keep our very special home base in the Idaho panhandle. Like so many other extended timers, we want to have our cake and eat it too! Based on our own experience, though, we conclude that it costs almost twice as much to live as a fulltimer if you keep a house.

Most years, we've left the house empty. We've made arrangements with a neighbor to check on the place regularly, including a weekly walk-through. We also notify the county sheriff's department of our absence. Of course, living in the country, our neighbors all know when we're gone and keep an eye on the place. As long as one has honest neighbors, that's great, but imagine the field day they could have if they decided to become burglars!

Some Personal Problems with Absentee Ownership

Our first winter away from home brought the supreme test of our ability to cope with the problems of absentee ownership. The neighbors who were checking the house called us in California to report that, to their horror, they had discovered the house flooded because a pipe had frozen and burst. The water pump had run for several days, pouring on the floor upstairs, then running down into the living room and on to the basement — an incredible mess. Water damage amounted to thousands of dollars; fortunately both house and furniture were insured. The emotional damage was even greater, but we survived and kept on RVing—with the water pump turned off now!

Renting Your Home

We tried renting the house to a well-interviewed and referenced "perfect couple." Guess what? We returned the next summer to dying trees, brown grass, and a dirty house that we were lucky to have at all because our "perfect couple" had nearly burned it down! After repairing the charred deck and side of the house, we decided that our first experience as landlords would be our last.

Then, for three years, we tried a different and very successful tack. A college student whom we knew well needed housing during the school year. We offered to swap him our home for maintenance of the same. This arrangement worked well until he graduated.

Our experiences, coupled with those we have heard about from others, have led us to these conclusions:

1. Renting out a house acquired specifically for this purpose may be a good way to make money, but renting out your *home* is not.
2. If you can find a responsible house sitter, great. However, be aware that what you see in that so-called responsible person may not be the reality. I remember the time we hired a female graduate student from a local college, a "certified prude," according to our youngest daughter upon meeting the house sitter (who was to be with her while we were on a month's trip). The day after we left, the "prude" made a deal with our daughter to alternate days for parties, moved her boyfriend in, and they both partied for the whole month.
3. Leaving a house vacant for long periods of time is risky—both from the standpoint of the danger of burglary or vandalism and the possibility of damage from broken pipes, wires, or gas lines. In short, keeping a house while RVing extensively is both an emotional and definitely a financial drain.
4. A final note: If you are leaving your house vacant,

check with your insurance agent to be sure that you are complying with their occupancy clauses.

Park-Model Trailers

An increasingly popular method of having a home-type home base is to own a park-model trailer, which is left in a favorite park — usually somewhere in the Sunbelt. Devotees of this lifestyle either buy or lease long-term lots on which they set up one of the new 400-square-foot units. These units can have a Florida (or Arizona) room of equal size added, giving a total of 800 square feet. Park models can be quite luxuriously equipped with all the conveniences and comforts of a small home. And the best part is that you still live in an RV park with RVer neighbors and related activities. Of course, you still keep the trailer or motorhome and leave when the mood strikes you, with your home base well protected behind the walls and gates of the park.

Chapter 6
What Do You Do with Your Possessions?

Most of us have a pack-rat instinct that makes us accumulate "things." Anyone who has lived in a house for many years, as most people who take up fulltiming have, has probably filled closets, drawers, shelves, the attic, the garage, and various other spaces with "stuff," usually called *possessions*. (Sometimes fancier words like *mementos of a lifetime, collectibles, memorabilia,* or *acquisitions* are used.) Included in this stuff is usually an accumulation of clothes that go back to wedding garb. What confounds me is why size-40 men still save size-34 pants that they haven't been able to get into for twenty years. Extreme optimism, perhaps? Call it what you will, I call most of what our houses are full of *crap!* Our homes are loaded with stuff that we don't use, don't look at, doesn't fit, is broke, is out of style, and certainly gives us no enjoyment. Why do we keep it? It's the pack-rat instinct that we have to divest ourselves of if we are to go fulltiming. But how do you get rid of it, you ask? I have several suggestions.

Sorting Your Possessions

The first is: Sort out the useful things you will need with you in your full-timing rig — clothes that you like, that *fit* you, and that you regularly wear, a few special pictures, selected kitchen and dining necessities, bedding, selected miscellaneous items, and, of course, some necessary tools and equipment from the garage. As an added means of control over what gets taken along, I recommend that each spouse have veto power over what the other wishes to take!

Getting Rid of the Rest

After you have intelligently packed your rig, offer what is left to your kids or close relatives. To create a *fair* situation, try this: Get a supply of play money and give the kids or relatives equal amounts. Then have an auction and let them establish their own values for your stuff. That way, each will get the items that are special to him or her and will make the values each gets comparable.

When your kids and close relatives have done their thing, invite grandkids, other relatives, friends, and neighbors to pick over what is left. End up with calling the Salvation Army or other favorite charity to pick up the items no one wants (be sure to get a receipt for your generous donation).

Of course, you can have a garage sale or auction, but this will deprive the kids of having some of the things that will remind them of "home." Besides, you can visit your stuff if the kids have it. You might even get to sit in *your* chair again — if your offspring will let you! Actually, the dollars you realize for most of your possessions won't be many. It's also painful to see your prized possessions go for peanuts. Emotionally, it's better to give it away to people you love and who will appreciate it.

Chapter 7
Kids, Grandkids, and Relatives

Some prospective fulltimers find giving up family too difficult — especially those who have routines where kids come over every Sunday for the day. The huge meals that Grandma spends all day fixing and which vanish in a few minutes, crying babies, kids getting into forbidden things in the garage, blaring TVs and radios — all these normal family get-togethers that become established Sunday routines for some people are too ingrained for some couples to surrender. The reality is that once you sell the house and hit the road, you can't have the family together every Sunday, and there will be extended periods when you won't see the grandchildren. Your contact with them will be by letter and telephone only. So if you are the kind who just has to have close physical contact with family, you won't be a very successful fulltimer.

Love Them and Leave Them

Most fulltimers don't need that kind of contact, yet they love their families just as much as anyone. They love, but are able to leave. Actually, they enjoy visiting their children, grandchildren, and other relatives at times of their own choosing. They like to pull up at an offspring's house, park in the driveway, and enjoy the children and grandchildren *on their terms*. They live in their own homes, go to bed when they prefer, have time to themselves if they wish (and can keep the grandkids out), and, above all, *leave when they wish*.

I am not making light of family ties and customs. It's just simply that some people don't consider thoroughly the consequences of being out of visiting range of family when they opt for the full-time lifestyle, and it creates problems. On the other hand, most of those who try fulltiming find they can balance out their need for family contact and the desire to live an exciting life on the road. Many also find the *quality* time they spend with family more than compensates for the *quantity* that was formerly the case.

Chapter 8
Keeping in Touch

Giving up life in a fixed place and taking to the road full time doesn't have to mean giving up contact with family and friends. Indeed, few of us are inclined to neglect our kids, grandkids, parents, and friends completely. Most of us on the road have developed patterns of communication that keep us within the swirl of family life, even though we aren't there in person.

By Mail

Thanks to our efficient U.S. Post Office, most of us are able to use the mail to keep in contact with others. Your post office will forward your mail for up to a year if you keep them informed of your address. However, in most cases, especially with those who travel extensively, this is usually not a satisfactory plan.

What works best and generally most effectively is to have all your mail sent to a reliable relative who can sort out what is important and what is junk. By phoning that person regularly, you can have your mail sent to wherever you are with the added bonus of being able to talk to him or her.

Mail-Forwarding Services

An alternative method, and one that is most widely used, is to use one of the many mail-forwarding services. Not only are they generally quite reliable, this plan doesn't create work and responsibility for someone in your family.

One of the better-known services is operated by the Good Sam Club. Typical of mail-forwarding services, there is a basic charge plus any postage required to forward mail to you. Times and procedures for notification vary somewhat with different mail-forwarding companies, as do the fees. Mail-forwarding services can be located through the "Services" classified ads in *Trailer Life* and *MotorHome* magazines and other RV-related publications.

Incidentally, fulltimers who travel a good deal usually have their mail forwarded to General Delivery in a town they choose on their route or to a campground where they expect to be long enough for the mail to get there. General Delivery should be used for small towns where your mail will be rather conspicuous. I can imagine the difficulty in receiving mail in a large city with many branch locations.

By Telephone

If one wishes to have daily communication with others, there are also phone-message services available. Most of them are offered by the same companies that do mail forwarding, Good Sam, for example, offers this service. Callers leave messages, which may be received by the subscriber by calling in at prescribed hours, or, as in the case of Good Sam's computerized service, at any time. Also, messages may be left for guests calling the service. As for costs, generally there is a basic charge, with additional charges based on the number of calls one receives or makes.

Nowadays, many fulltimers have cellular phones in their rigs. The advantage is that the service makes you immediately available to anyone who wants you as long as you are within a cellular service zone; the disadvantages are:

1. If you travel extensively, you won't always be in an area with service.
2. The cost is rather high.

Until very recently, we had rejected the idea of having a cellular phone in our motorhome because we are so often where there is no service—and air time charges are so high. However, both of those factors are changing. Wider coverage and cheaper rates are altering the picture. Also, due to the emergency open heart surgery I required last year while on the road, we have decided that the need for quick communications outweighs the expense of having a cellular phone. Due to the relatively high cost of calls, we seldom use our phone, but we are comforted by the fact that it is there if we need it.

Since mail and message services are generally offered in states where there are tax advantages (either sales or income), I would recommend that prospective fulltimers carefully investigate and consider what would be best for them if they plan to use that address as their legal one. (And don't forget the necessity to comply with state laws regarding residence.)

So, as you can see, there's no need for fulltimers to pull the communications plug on their families and friends just because they have unplugged their connections to a particular piece of real estate.

Chapter 9
Handling Financial Affairs

Can you have a bank and carry on regular banking services while on the road? You bet you can. And it's all quite simple.

Banking by Mail

Deposits may be made by mail. Banks provide deposit envelopes and deposit slips for that purpose. We've been mailing our checks in to our banks for over ten years and have never had a dime lost. To make depositing even easier, you can arrange to have all regular checks, especially government or company pensions, *directly* deposited. Then you don't have to go through the receiving, endorsing, and mailing procedure.

Handling on-the-Road Expenses

Since most of us paid bills by mail even before taking up RVing, there's really no change there. So for normal banking purposes, the only change is mail-in deposits.

Paying regular travel and living expenses on the road is best done by credit card. One of the major credit cards (with as high a limit as possible to take care of major emergencies) and an automatic teller machine (ATM) card (both can be combined nowadays) are really all one needs. Most businesses take plastic, and for getting cash on the road all one needs is the ATM card. It can keep dollars in your pocket with a minimum of difficulty. We use credit cards and pay our monthly bills in full before interest charges accrue, so there's no extra expense for us. If you don't normally pay all your charge card bills before interest charges accrue, you should shop around for the best interest rates (they vary widely). Our ATM card costs a dollar for each use. Actually, the only significant expenses connected with using credit cards are that most gas stations give a discount for cash, and many campgrounds won't give a Good Sam discount if a card is used. Other than these two instances, cards are the same as cash.

Some companies and banks issue special types of cards, such as debit cards, but except for a few special cases, I see no need for them.

Handling Tax Payments on the Road

I often hear RVers say in March that they have to go home to do taxes. That's totally unnecessary for most people. Unless you're in a business with extensive records, you can do it all by mail. Our taxes aren't exactly overcomplicated, but neither are they simple, and we haven't been home for taxes in a dozen years. We simply keep our records with us and add receipts and other documentation as we go along. Then at tax time, I sort everything out, do all the preliminary figuring, and ship the information off to our accountant in California. He puts it all on the proper forms and sends it to us for signatures (and sometimes more money). I'm sure that some people have need to discuss their financial affairs at great length with their accountants, but, in most cases, it is just taking up the accountant's time (which, believe me, he is charging for).

In short, there is seldom any need for a person to be actually present to handle normal financial matters. It can usually be done by mail and telephone.

Chapter 10
Health Care

The Golden Years, the Senior Citizen Era, the More Mature Years, call the retirement period what you will, it's usually when most RVers begin fulltiming. Having the time and opportunity to do so generally doesn't come until after one falls into the category sociologists call simply "old age." And, unfortunately, it's a time when human bodies are more prone to get out of whack, or those that are already malfunctioning get worse. It's a time when the term *health care* takes on additional significance. Therefore, it may become a major concern for those who are considering being away from normal health-care facilities and, especially, their own doctors.

Since the variety and severity of health problems is almost infinite, it is difficult to generalize about how to approach the question of health care on the road. However, there are some basic preparations most of us can make that will enable us to cope better with our ills, both present and future.

Preparing for Health Care on the Road

Probably the most important element in health care is to know what your problems are, if any, and to give them proper treatment — hence the need for regular and thorough physical examinations. *Regular* has different meanings in different situations and with different doctors. Some physicians advocate annual checkups. Others suggest more frequent exams, and still others recommend complete physicals only every other year. Whatever the term, the point is to keep aware of your condition so oncoming ailments can be identified and treated early and preparations for further treatments can be planned for.

Not only should you have good knowledge of your physical condition, you should have medical records with you as you travel. Any doctor nowadays will make copies of your record and give it to you. With it in hand, you are in a position to save both time and money when you stop for treatment or assistance at any doctor's office, clinic, or hospital in your travels. Incidentally, these records should be kept in a fire-proof box along with your other important papers.

If you take pills or other medications, you should always keep a good supply on hand. Also, have prescriptions for refills with you if you are going to be away from your regular doctor(s) for long periods of time. However, you should be aware that laws vary from state to state, so a prescription written by a doctor in one may not be honored in another.

Walk-in Clinics

One of the big changes in availability of medical services has been the advent of "walk-in" clinics. Like the fast-food industry, you can now almost get drive-through treatment for less-serious health problems. Most cities and large towns have them. I've even seen them in relatively small towns, especially those with heavy concentrations of older people.

Know First Aid

Everyone should have some basic knowledge of first aid and a reasonably complete first-aid kit. We also carry a blood-pressure monitor that requires no special skill to operate. Knowledge of cardiopulmonary resuscitation (CPR) is very important. Many rally programs include free CPR lessons, and they are also offered by many city agencies, such as fire departments and organizations like the Red Cross.

Handling Major Health Emergencies

Looking at the grim side for a moment, let's ask what you do in extreme health emergencies while on the road. Assume it becomes necessary to have major surgery with a fairly long period of recuperation and frequent attention from a doctor. Actually, being in an RV can be the easiest and best situation you could ask for. If there's no nearby RV park, almost any hospital will allow you to park on their parking lot (some even provide spaces with hookups). So you don't have to go through the ordeal of driving from a home miles away to go see the doctor. You're there! And in case of emergency flare-ups, you're only seconds away from the experts. Not long ago, a friend of ours had a heart attack while in a strange city. Quadruple bypass surgery was performed. Rather than have his wife drive to their hometown, they spent the period of recuperation in a campground just a few blocks from the hospital *without the disruption of well-wishers.*

Even on a grimmer side, death is always a possibility while on the road. Prepare for this eventuality just as you would prepare for it if you lived in a house. Wills should be made (with copies in the fireproof box), as well as family agreements and provisions for the handling of remains.

Maintaining a Regular Health Program

The last, but certainly not the least, important recommendation for the best in health care is proper eating and exercise. It is my observation that, as a group, RVers enjoy better health than folks of similar ages in the general population. The reason must be that they exercise more — walking, bicycling, dancing, and swimming. Many snowbird parks offer formal aerobics classes and other types of exercises. All fulltimers should have a regular exercise regimen, be careful of what they eat, and pay attention to their weight. It's so easy to get into bad health habits when you're "jus' loafin' "; it may not be easier, but it's a lot better to be fit.

We find that a morning walk of two miles, regardless of where we are, goes part of the way toward keeping us reasonably fit. In bad weather, we use our foldaway cross-country skier. Actually, it does double duty because we can watch the news as we exercise. We also keep bathroom scales handy to get a reading every morning. If our weight is up, it's a diet-powder milkshake for lunch!

The main thing is to be conscious of your health and conscientious about maintaining an ongoing health program.

Chapter 11
Insurance

You can be fully insured in all respects as a fulltimer, but some companies either don't insure people who do not live in permanent houses or their coverages aren't adequate. Consequently, your on-the-road insurance shopping may include more than comparisons of rates and services. You may have to include the question: Do you insure fulltimers?

Vehicle Insurance

Vehicle insurance for your rig, for example, is generally the biggest problem. Many companies simply won't insure vehicles that don't have a regular home address. In fact, although I'm sure that there are others, the only two that I know for sure that do insure fulltimers are the Good Sam Club and Alexander & Alexander (see various articles in *Highways, Trailer Life, MotorHome,* and other RV publications). These sources also provide liability and homeowners' coverage. A great thing about these companies is that their programs were designed for us active RVers and address some of the needs that we didn't have when we lived in houses. Incidentally, make absolutely sure that your vehicle's contents are insured at *replacement value.* Also, only recently, some companies have begun offering *replacement* insurance on RVs.

Emergency Road Service

A special kind of insurance that every fulltimer needs is emergency road service. Having a breakdown in a car is bad enough, but having a breakdown in a large RV can be disastrous. Even changing a tire on a motorhome can be beyond the capability of some RVers, and having to be towed a hundred miles can devastate a budget. Although some auto clubs cover RVs, it would be wise to check your policy before a need to use the coverage arises. I can say from personal experience that Good Sam's Emergency Road Service is great. Our personal test came just last year when our motorhome burned up while we were traveling. My concern for removal of the burned-out hulk (a total loss) was quickly alleviated by one phone call. Not only did the service cover the entire cost of loading and hauling off a mountain of debris, it was done promptly and thoroughly, without hassle.

Health and Life Insurance

While most health insurance is still valid after you take up fulltiming, it would be a wise decision to check with your company to see what their requirements are for obtaining service. It could be that there are some difficulties in handling the paperwork while on the road. Again, I suggest that you investigate Good Sam's plan, which, as with their vehicle insurance, is designed especially for RVers — including fulltimers. Of course, Medicare benefits and procedures aren't affected by changes in lifestyle.

Generally, life-insurance policies aren't affected by moving from a fixed place to a life on the road. Still, check it out with your agent.

As with any insurance in any condition, my advice is to use as few companies as possible for all your needs. If you can get everything you need and deal with only one agent or company, it simplifies things when the time comes to reap some of the benefits of the premiums you've paid.

My final advice: Regardless of who your insurers are and what coverage they provide, it is crucial to take your insurance policies and forms with you in a fireproof box.

Chapter 12
Pack Your Papers

A fact of life (and death) in this age is that we live and die fully documented. Most of the aspects of daily living are in some way connected with written records. Indeed, such documents play so important a role in our lives that if we should suddenly lose them all, I'm not sure we could function very long.

We vary individually in our paper needs. Some are basic for everyone, but others are essential for select individuals. Let's take a look at some of the various categories of common documents.

Vehicle Titles and Registrations

Obviously, every RVer has vehicle title and registration documents, and they should be with most of us in our rigs. Registrations are always required by state laws. The need for a title may occur only infrequently; however, there's always the possibility of running into a deal on a new RV that is irresistible, or one of those horrible occasions when machines give up their ghosts and you are forced to get something new. In short, you must have a title at trading time.

Birth Certificates and/or Passports

You never know when you're going to have to provide verification of citizenship. When going to Mexico or Canada, for example, it may not be needed; it's nice to have proof of citizenship handy if it is. On the other hand, if you suddenly decide to take a trip to a country that requires a passport, it's absolutely crucial to have your birth certificate with you so you can get one.

Financial Records

Papers having to do with bank accounts, mortgages, notes, stocks, and bonds may come in handy at any time while you're traveling, so they should also be with you. For example, if you wish to cash a certificate of deposit (CD), it won't do you much good if the certificate is in a safe deposit box in a far-away city. Tax records, too, should be carried along, just in case the IRS wants to have a discussion with you. Also, these records might be necessary for credit purposes (like when you get the urge for a new rig and your bank account is a bit low).

I have already mentioned insurance papers, wills, and medical records, which together with the preceding should be carried with you in a fireproof safe or box. The Sentry Company makes a line of various-size boxes that are modestly priced and are carried in most discount stores.

Bear this in mind: Your "important" papers have little importance if you don't have them with you when you need them most.

Chapter 13
Pets

I understand well the feelings of those who wish to take their pets with them. We love animals and always had pets when we lived a "regular" life, but we decided at the beginning of our extended RVing not to take them with us. We know that we can't care for a dog or cat properly living the way we do, and we aren't able or willing to change. We're often away from our motorhome for many hours at a time. Sometimes we even have to make side trips by air and stay at hotels. Pets simply don't mix with our style of living.

But if you have pets that you've grown very attached to, you'll undoubtedly enjoy them enormously during your many hours together on the road.

Some Considerations for Pet Owners

If you have an animal, be it dog, cat, bird, or whatever, there are few reasons other than those you personally may have for not being able to take your pet with you. True, a few campgrounds and RV parks don't permit them at all, but generally they are allowed—with the normal restrictions.

However, the big questions are those that only you can answer: Are you willing to give the pet the attention he or she requires? For instance, are you prepared to stop when Fifi needs to stop? Will you be willing to restrict your time out of the RV to fit your pet's demands? Are you willing to take care of your pet properly, considering other RVers and rules of RV parks and campgrounds? You have to face the fact that an animal *restricts* your activities tremendously. For instance, you have arrived at a city like Boston, and you want to tour all the historical places. *You* can take tour buses, but your dog can't. So what happens to Fifi while you are on an eight-hour tour? I guarantee you, if I happen to be your neighbor RVer and your dog barks all day, you will hear from me in no uncertain terms when you return — as will the park manager.

Consider Your Neighbors

Without intending to raise a controversy, I'd like to emphasize here that inconsiderate pet owners create some of the major problems for campground owners. They're the ones who disobey campground and common-sense rules, the ones who believe that their dogs are exempt from the leash rules, that Fifi's doo-doo is okay anywhere she feels the urge to deposit it and that there's no need for them to pick it up, those who feel that it's all right for their dogs to "express themselves" by barking whenever they feel like it, or those who believe that their pet's behavior is always perfectly accepted by others. I'm amazed at how many apparently kind, intelligent, and generally considerate people are completely irrational in their attitudes about acceptable pet behavior. In fact, some have become so confused in their thinking that they believe everyone who objects to their permissiveness about objectionable pet behavior is wrong. Some even refuse to believe their pet is capable of unacceptable behavior.

Last year, I had the misfortune to encounter a pair of the most ridiculous owners I've ever met. They parked beside me in a campground that had clearly stated leash rules. However, they allowed their Doberman to roam as he pleased outside their coach. On the second day, as I got out of *my* car in *my* space, and just as I put my left leg out the door, the dog rushed up and grabbed my leg. Fortunately, I had on heavy jeans and the bite didn't break the skin, but it did hurt. I yelled. The dog's owner was outside his coach, and he asked what the matter was. When I told him, "Your dog bit me," his reply was, "But my dog doesn't bite." That scene was repeated as the lady appeared in the door. Unbelievable! Neither could comprehend the reality. Obviously, to them, I was making something up. They're the kind of people who make life difficult for all dog owners.

Incidentally, I could have made life difficult for them with a lawsuit, but I didn't. However, I did report the incident to the campground owner, who immediately evicted them — still protesting that their dog doesn't bite!

Most nonpet owners respect others' rights to have pets, but they expect their rights to be respected in return.

In short, there's little reason for you not to take your pet if you want to; but, if you do, there's every reason for you to take care of it properly.

Chapter 14
Weapons

Without the backing of an objective study, I think I would be safe in saying that at least 75 percent of the RVs on the road have some kind of gun in them — most often a handgun. It is a fact of American life that most people have a gun or guns in their houses, and mobile houses are no exception.

Legal or Not?

While it is not my intent to get embroiled in the right-to-keep-and-bear-arms controversy, I think we should all be aware of the fact that having a firearm in one's possession can get a person into trouble. The federal government, all states, many counties, and many municipalities have gun laws. Unfortunately, those laws aren't uniform, and what may be legal in one place may not be legal in another.

Although we may claim that our homes on wheels are just as much our "castles" as our homes on the ground and that we are entitled to have firearms in our homes, not all law-enforcement officers, judges, and juries agree. In fact, I recently heard from a person who ended up with a felony conviction and a very stiff sentence for having a "concealed weapon in a motor vehicle." The judge didn't care that the woman claimed the van was her home; to him, it was a vehicle. A state appellate court upheld her conviction. Whether you or I or anyone else agrees or disagrees with the court's decision is irrelevant. The fact is she was accused of having a concealed weapon in a vehicle and was convicted. And another fact is the same thing can happen to any of us if we carry handguns.

The problem is *handguns* — not rifles or shotguns. There

are few laws restricting the carrying of either rifles or shotguns, so my suggestion is to avoid the possibility of problems with the law and carry either a rifle or shotgun — that is, if you feel you must carry a gun at all. I particularly recommend the latter, especially a pump shotgun. Stop to think about it: You're a robber prowling around someone's trailer in the middle of a dark night when all at once you hear the thwack-thwack of a shell being chambered into a pump shotgun. What will you do? Run, of course — what any sensible person would do under the circumstances. The sound alone is enough to scare most intruders off. Besides, if you're going to shoot at someone in the dark, aren't your chances of hitting them a heck of a lot better with a shotgun than a pistol?

Firearms in Other Countries

RVers traveling to Canada and Mexico would be wise to investigate the laws of these countries carefully before attempting to take any kind of firearm into them. It can be done, but there are regulations, which, if broken, can create *big* problems, especially in Mexico, where the rights of the accused differ widely from those we know.

Know How to Use Your Weapon

Finally, if you are going to carry a weapon, presumably for protection, know how to use it, and be very aware of the fact that if you threaten someone with it, you may end up using it. The consequences for that can be very serious.

Chapter 15
Membership Campgrounds

A wonderful aspect of fulltiming is that one's options of how to go about it are numerous and varied. However, that makes tough decisions necessary at times, decisions which may directly affect your pocketbook.

A question that I am frequently asked is: What do you think about campground memberships? My answer is always something to the effect that they're great for some people and of no value to others.

I have questioned membership owners all over the country and usually ask attendees at my seminars what they think. Answers seem to be equally divided between whether they are happy or unhappy with their purchases. Many RVers find memberships are wise investments for both financial and emotional reasons. Some say their membership program fits right in with their preferences and that they plan their travels to fit within the membership framework. Others tell me that they were "fast-talked" into something they can't or don't use.

Travel First—Join Later

I would suggest that if you're a beginning fulltimer you should get some experience on the road before investing in any membership, especially if you're the type who has a very indefinite travel program. After a few months on the road, you might decide that structured travel, that is having to stay at specific places and conform with specific reservation rules, is not to your taste. On the other hand, you might decide that the plus side, particularly the security provided by reservations and quality of facilities, far outweighs any inconveniences created by regulations.

Consider the Cost

Most experienced fulltimers take a hard look at the economics of memberships. With prices often in the $4,000-plus price range, plus annual fees, it should be obvious that from a financial standpoint, it takes a lot of nights of camping to reach the break-even point. One must also consider that the cash invested draws no interest as it would if it were in a savings account; a financed membership *costs* interest!

But saving money isn't the only objective of memberships. Sometimes the features offered by a particular program fit right into one's notions of RVing. Some people like going to the same places regularly, where they have friends and activities they especially like. People who buy memberships to get these features are buying *fun* — and there's no way to put a price tag on that.

Another factor you should investigate before plunking down thousands of dollars is the financial strength of the company selling the memberships. A hard fact is that several membership companies have gone bankrupt in recent years, and others are in dire financial straits.

My suggestion is simply that you consider carefully what you are getting before you give up your hard-earned bucks. And a special tip: If a salesman is putting on the pressure for you to get a "fabulous offer good only *today*," wonder to yourself what is so special about today that makes the same price no good tomorrow. Sleep on it. Then make your decision on what's best for you.

Chapter 16
RV Clubs

Many fulltimers find that membership in an RV club is a very desirable — even indispensible — aspect of RVing. While most of the time they're on their own, club members usually make it a point to attend rallies several times a year, where they can visit with old friends and make new ones. In fact, most fulltimers look upon those get-togethers as reunions, where they can savor a sense of family and community.

Finding a Club

There are many different kinds of RV clubs. Dealers sometimes form their own; fraternal orders, large companies, and churches frequently have camping clubs. Many RV manufacturers sponsor "name-brand" clubs, some of which are company owned and managed, while others are independent. Some clubs are huge; for example, Family Motor Coach Association (FMCA) has a membership approaching 100,000. Of course, its membership is limited to motorhome owners.

The largest group of all is the Good Sam Club, which now has over 950,000 members and is expected to hit the million mark in the 1990s. With its enormous size, it, like FMCA, is broken up into regions, which in turn are broken up into state chapters, and then into local chapters. Most meetings take place at the local level, with one state rally held each year; a huge international rally is also held each year. Most club members participate at the local level, but some are active at both state and national levels. You can participate any way you prefer.

Reasons for Joining an RV Club

Let's take a look at some of the benefits of RV club membership.

Fellowship
Clubs bring people together, people with at least two basic interests — RVing and other people. Other interests may vary enormously, but when they're together at rallies, they're all birds of a feather, and the rally is viewed as only one big party.

Education
There's no better place to get a degree in RVing than in a club. If you ask questions and listen, you can hear the answers to anything and everything about the RV lifestyle and the equipment we use. Some of that information comes from other RVers, but it also comes from seminars put on by various experts — some on technical matters, others on lifestyle concerns. Rallies are excellent places for novice fulltimers to learn.

Caravans and Tours
Many clubs, particularly name-brand motorhome clubs, plan several caravans or tours each year. Participants pay a fee up front, and a wagonmaster takes care of all the details — including overnight stopping places, some meals, and entertainment. It's a particularly good way to venture forth to places you might be afraid to tackle alone.

Discounts and Special Benefits
Some of the large clubs have arranged for member discounts at various facilities and on RV accessories and services. The Good Sam Club is particularly oriented toward these benefits. Their program provides for discounts at hundreds of campgrounds, RV-supply stores, and service centers.

There's something for almost every fulltimer in an RV club. Try it — you may like it!

Chapter 17
Snowbird Roosts

They might have different views on the right way to RV, but there is one maxim fulltimers all agree on: When it gets cold up north, go south! Disagreements are only about *where* to go in the south.

Following the Sun

The Sun Belt stretches from the Atlantic to the Pacific and includes from nine to thirteen states, depending on who's calling the shots. Of these, four states probably get seventy-five percent or more of the RV-snowbird business: Florida, Texas, Arizona, and California. When a snowbird says he's going south, the odds are that he will be going to one of these states.

To further narrow the bounds of "snowbird roosts," those who go to Florida will probably land in the central part of the state or on the Gulf Coast. Those who winter in Texas generally go to the lower Rio Grande Valley, a less-than-100-mile stretch of land reaching from McAllen to South Padre Island. The Phoenix area, generally, and Mesa, specifically, are the most popular spots for Arizona birds, but there is a large contingent in the Yuma area, too. Southern California birds generally settle in Riverside, Imperial, and San Diego counties. So, despite the fact that the Sun Belt is indeed a large geographical area, RV snowbirds follow the old dictum "birds of a feather flock together"—and end up in big bunches in relatively few places.

Choosing Your Place in the Sun

Margie and I have tried all the popular snowbird roosts, and we have our favorite: Yuma. We like its small-town atmosphere, generally modest park prices, adequate shopping facilities, and absolutely super desert climate. Plus, quite a few of our special friends winter there. However, I would not presume to recommend it to everyone. The fact that there are several big roosts and a great many small ones indicates the variety of personal preferences. Each place has plenty of pluses, and, unfortunately, each has some minuses. You can hear pros and cons about every one of them, and every view has elements of truth.

Snowbirds have a tendency to go directly south; that is, Easterners tend to go to Florida, Midwesterners to Texas and Florida, and Westerners to Arizona and California. In spite of the fact they have all the time in the world, they usually opt for places nearest to their former homes. That's unfortunate for them, in a way, because I suspect that some would prefer other areas if they were only willing to travel a couple of days longer. That's why I recommend fulltimers try all the major snowbird areas before concluding they've found the right one.

Common Aspects of Snowbird Areas

Basically, most areas popular with snowbirds have a number of characteristics in common. The most important, of course, is relatively warm winters. I say *relatively* because all areas get unusually cold or otherwise have disagreeable weather at times. For example, I'm writing this page in mid-December in Lake Wales, Florida, where the temperature has been in the mid-eighties all week, and saw on the news that it snowed in Phoenix.

However, there are other factors that make places popular with snowbirds. Among them are a varied selection of RV parks with a wide range of prices; good, reasonably priced restaurants; plenty of golf courses; good fishing (or other outdoor activities); shopping; light traffic conditions; adequate medical facilities; and special areas to see and activities to do.

Individual preferences may make other requirements more important. For example, most boondockers seek only a private spot in the sun.

A word of caution to novice snowbirds: Don't expect in a short, few-day visit to get a completely true picture of an area. It takes time and some "soaking up." A person who has the misfortune to stop at any snowbird area when the wind is blowing, the mercury is down, the rain is torrential, or the bugs are fierce may totally misjudge the long-term advantages of that area. Bear in mind that *all* snowbird areas have the best winter weather in the nation, but *all* also have their bad moments.

In short, try every area and give each a fair shake. After all, if every one of these areas is popular with thousands of "birds," they must have found something good. Maybe you need look only a little longer.

Chapter 18
The Cost of Fulltiming

Like the cost of "regular" living, there's no way to put a definite price tag on full-time RV living. Actually, it is a very democratic lifestyle — you can make it on any amount you set for yourself. I've talked with people who are getting by on less than $500 per month, and I know people who apparently have unlimited bank accounts.

It is quite obvious that not everyone will travel and live the same way, although many of the benefits of fulltiming are common to all, whether they're rich or poor, or whether their rigs are worth a thousand dollars or a hundred thousand. The sun's rays don't beam any warmer on the man with a larger bank account; a rich man can't enjoy a national park or a historical monument any more than a poor fellow. However, they can eat differently, they can stay in different kinds of parks, and they can roam farther.

The "Big Four" Budget Factors

The cost of fulltiming can be geared to almost any financial level by the control of the "Big Four" budget factors for an RVer:

1. The cost of the RV
2. The number of miles you travel
3. The parks you stay in
4. What you spend on entertainment and other nonessentials, such as admissions to attractions, eating out, gifts, souvenirs, booze, etc.

Incidentally, uncontrollable factors, such as insurance,

taxes, medical care, or RV repairs, are in addition to the four preceding categories.

I won't presume at this point to present sample formal budgets. There are just too many variables, as well as the fact that most people simply don't use formal budgets. People of "full-timing age" have generally developed patterns of spending over the years that fit their incomes, and they simply jockey the amounts around a bit to fit their new incomes and lifestyle. What I do want to emphasize is, in that jockeying, you need to take into extra consideration the "Big Four" cost factors when you're trying to achieve a balance between what you've got and what you want.

The Cost of a Rig

Obviously, you can spend any amount of money you want on an RV — ranging from a few hundred to several hundred thousand dollars. In fact, looking out my window as I write this, five spaces away and directly in my view is a Prevost Liberty conversion motorhome that cost someone between $400,000 and $500,000. Right down the street is a small Sprite travel trailer with an older tow car that must have a present combined value of under $10,000. Yet both owners are enjoying the same kind of hookups, the same amenities of the resort, and the same camaraderie of other RVers. And the 85-degree sun is beaming exactly the same on each party! Whether or not they are fulltiming, I don't know, but my illustration shows that the rig's use and the enjoyment by their owners is the same regardless of how much their rigs cost. My point is that you don't have to have any particular kind of RV or one of any particular value. You buy what you *want* if you have deep pockets; you buy what you *can afford* if you're like most of us.

A consideration you should bear in mind about the size and value of the rig you choose: Licenses, insurance premiums, and operating costs are directly related to those factors. Ask yourself if you want the long-term costs of whatever RV you choose. In the same vein, consider carefully the financial impact of monthly payments if you start fulltiming with a financed rig. (Due to the importance and expense of the purchase of a full-time rig, Chapter 19 is devoted to this topic.)

Once you have the rig—as most fulltimers do when they start—you must cope with the remaining three Big Four factors. They are with you as long as you are on the road. Every day, sometimes several times a day, you must make decisions that affect your budget. You probably will develop your own methods of control, but I advise you to keep your eyes and ears open for new ideas. There are always new lessons to be learned, often from other RVers.

The Cost of Fuel

Gas costs are controlled primarily by the amount of driving you do. Some RVers travel many thousands of miles each year (we do), while others move infrequently and only short distances. For example, we criss-cross the nation every year to give our seminars at RV shows. Fortunately, we can combine RVing and work, but it does require an exceptional amount of driving. At the other extreme, we know many RVers who move only twice a year—once south and once north.

With fuel costs what they are now, and the possibility that they will go even higher, the miles you travel are indeed dear. At prices ranging up to as much as $1.60 a gallon in some regions (usually in the west), a motorhome or tow vehicle giving eight or ten miles per gallon makes the cost of an extra 1,000 miles significant.

There are three ways to soften the gas-bill blow: don't drive as much, get a smaller, lightweight rig, and shop fuel prices carefully.

Since most fulltimers prefer large RVs, the first procedure is the primary method of control. Actually, that isn't bad. One of the major objectives of fulltiming is to *see* things, so limiting miles on the road gives more time to "stop and smell the roses." In fact, there might even be a formula one can apply: *Cover one half the miles you planned and get twice the enjoyment you anticipated.* Or, *Enjoyment of fulltiming increases in direct proportion to decreases in the miles driven.*

Exercising option number two can be very effective. I daresay that fellow down the way with the Prevost gets no more than five miles per gallon, whereas the fellow with the Sprite may get fifteen, eighteen, or even twenty miles per gallon. In short, one way is four or five times as costly as the other.

When you're squirting a gallon of fuel through your carburetor every seven or eight miles, a few cents per gallon make a big difference over a thousand miles. So it pays to shop for gas, especially if you have a huge tank. My motorhome tank usually takes eighty to eighty-four gallons at a fillup, so five cents a gallon means four bucks!

Follow these steps in buying gas:

1. Plan on stopping in a city or town. As a rule, but certainly not always, the more isolated a station is, the higher the price.
2. Sometimes it pays to get away from the major offramps from freeways. I've noted that in some towns with few offramps, gas is higher at the stations at these places than it is down the street.
3. Always note prices at two or three stations before pulling in. It hurts to discover gas selling for a dime a gallon less just a few miles down the road.
4. Keep a record of towns or states where gas is regularly priced lower, and plan gas stops there when possible.
5. Finally, pay cash if there is a difference in cash and credit prices.

The Cost of a Campground

The third very controllable budget factor concerns the places where you spend your nights. For example, some RV resorts have fees that range up to $40 a night, but boondocking is free. Four nights at the former means $160 out of your pocket; at the latter, you spend nothing. Extreme though these cases are, they illustrate clearly my point that *you* decide how much you will spend on space rent.

On an average, overnight fees at RV parks are about $15. Some are a few dollars more and others a few less. Qualities definitely aren't the same. Last week, we paid $11 a night at a passable place, $12 at another. Both were mediocre: the hookups were adequate, but the interior streets were rutted, the spaces had no paved or grassy patios, and there were no amenities except for small clubhouses. This week we're at a lovely resort in Florida with concrete pads and patios, manicured grounds, and every conceivable amenity— pools, clubhouses with exercise equipment, and card rooms. But we're paying $25 a night!

Again, if you plug into your budget the $15 figure, you'll generally find yourself being realistic. Incidentally, campground guides (see *Trailer Life Campground & RV Services Directory*) list RV rates along with other information about each park or campground.

There are several ways to bring nightly fees down. The first is simple: Join the Good Sam Club and take advantage of ten-percent discounts at the hundreds of campgrounds that are commercial members. Another savings, when hookups are extra, don't pay for anything you don't need. Also, take advantage of advertised specials, such as one night free with a paid night (but be prepared for a possible sales pitch at some places). And by all means, remember that weekly and monthly rates are much less expensive than a per-night basis. Finally, investigate membership campgrounds *very carefully* to see if they offer any programs that will save you money (see Chapter 15, "Campground Memberships").

The Cost of Nonessentials

The fourth controllable full-timing budget factor might be called miscellaneous nonessential purchases. I include in this category meals not prepared in your rig, that is, eating or dining out.

I make a distinction between *eating* out and *dining* out. In the latter, you might go to a grand restaurant, be seated by a maitre d' at an elegantly set table, start with cocktails and appetizers, have steak and lobster, a bottle of wine, a flaming dessert, and finally an after-dinner drink, which will be followed by another sizzling item— a bill for over $100 for two people. Now that's *dining* out.

On the other hand, that same couple can drop in at Denny's and get a reasonable five-course dinner from the senior citizen's menu (at $3.59 each at this writing), pay with a ten-dollar bill, and get enough change to pick up a bottle of Ripple on the way home for that after-dinner nip. That is *eating* out. And it doesn't take a mathematical genius to choose your budget niche.

Obviously, there are dozens of other ways to save a buck, depending on your particular habits. Since I can't recall offhand any fulltimers I've met who seemed in dire financial straits, I can only assume that apparently most have learned the lessons they need to about their personal budgets.

The Total Cost of Fulltiming

I'm frequently asked how much the average person spends on fulltiming, and I offer only a ballpark figure: somewhere in the vicinity of $1,500 per month. Probably eighty percent of the fulltimers that I ask tell me that is what they find sufficient in their cases. That figure does not include major purchases, such as a new RV or a new car. Nor does it include the support of a house somewhere. I've arrived at that figure after talking to scores of fulltimers. It's interesting to note that many people feel this figure is high, while many others feel it is too low. As I've said before, each individual gears spending to his or her income, or, as I have put it somewhat facetiously, we spend what we make just as we did in "regular" life.

But no matter whether one spends $500 or $5,000 a month, many of the joys of fulltiming aren't measured in how much is spent. Nature's bounty, for example, is generally free. The elation and satisfaction of seeing Yellowstone Falls is no greater for the rich man than for one who is poor; the breakers on the Oregon coast pound no louder or higher for the couple with a $250,000 motorhome than for those two with a homemade camper on an old truck. Maybe the wealthier people can *dine* out regularly on fancy foods, but they can't enjoy their dinners any more than people who roast weiners over a campfire at the campsite by a mountain stream. In short, *whether or not* to take up fulltiming doesn't usually depend on your finances; *how you do it* definitely does.

Chapter 19
The Fulltiming Rig

The perspective from which one chooses a fulltiming rig may differ drastically from the perspective one uses in selecting a rig for recreational use. In the latter case, you are seeking temporary shelter away from home during vacations; in the former, the object of your search is the home that must provide all the functions of the house you give up to take to the road. Unlike recreational use, which may involve inconveniences that can be overlooked because they are of short duration, fulltiming means 365 days a year with one's equipment — be it convenient or inconvenient, comfortable or uncomfortable, practical or impractical, loved or hated. If you fail to properly judge your needs when purchasing a full-time rig, you may have nagging regrets you didn't make a wiser choice before handing over your money.

Some Rules for Choosing an RV

The saying "different strokes for different folks" is nowhere more meaningful than with people who are buying full-time rigs. Even though there is a general lifestyle labeled *fulltiming*, the fact is that there are many variations on how one lives full time in an RV. Those variations make it difficult, even impossible, to designate one size, one floorplan, one style as the perfect rig. That perfection has to be achieved within the limitations and requirements individuals impose upon themselves with their personal needs and wishes.

However, there are some general rules I believe to be quite valid, regardless of one's personal preferences. My rules don't provide specifics, but, hopefully, they will provide some basis for judgments.

Size

Buy as large as you want, that is, what "grabs you" in terms of comfort and livability, as long as there is no valid reason why you shouldn't buy that large. For example, you may *want* a 40 footer, but you know it won't be practical for traveling in the mountainous country where you plan to spend a lot of time. Obviously, that kind of use precludes the use of a large rig. In another example, you would like a 40 footer, but you are afraid to drive or tow an RV that large. No doubt you could, but if doing so would give you white knuckles everytime you got behind the wheel, your trips would be miserable. That's a good reason *not* to get a 40 footer. On the other hand, if you really *want* a huge RV, and you can't think of any reason not to have one, then by all means go for it. The fact that someone told someone else who told you a 40 footer is too big is no more a reason not to get a unit that size than the advice from someone who says a 27 footer is the perfect size.

Quality

In cases when there is a decision hangup over size or quality, and there is no serious financial question, tend to go larger and with the best quality. In over thirty years of RVing, nineteen of them while an RV dealer, I can't recall many instances of owners expressing regret at buying too large a rig or one that was too high in quality. On the other hand, I have heard many laments over owning an RV that was too small or of an inferior quality.

Options

In selecting options, my recommendation is simply: *Get every option offered unless there is a reason not to.* Examples of "reasons not to" include such things as the following: If you never watch television in bed, don't get a TV in the bedroom; or, if air conditioning gives you pneumonia, don't buy air conditioners. As with size, I've heard many owners wish they had ordered certain options at the time of purchase — especially as they go through the inconvenience and extra expense of adding them later. Most options are better installed and lower priced at the factory.

Livability

In making a final selection, regardless of the RV type or size, I recommend very strongly the "livability test." *When you have narrowed your choices down to what you think is the right rig, do a mock "live-in," that is, go through each aspect of living in the coach.* Visualize using each section as you would use it if you lived in it. Sit in the chairs and try to determine how you would feel after watching television or reading for three or four hours. Don't you do that every evening? Sit at the dining table. Do your legs and back fit? You're going to be in that position three times a day! Test the bed. Does it fit your back? Your height? Use the bathroom. Do you fit in the shower? Can you use the lavatory without spilling water all over? Sit on the commode. Does it fit? Check the kitchen extra carefully — go through the motions of cooking a meal and taking all the items you need from the various storage places. Is there room for everything? Is the counter large enough? Check all the storage places inside and out. Do you have the room and carrying capacity (Gross Vehicle Weight Rating or GVWR) for everything you wish to take along? Make sure each part does its job the way you want it for the 365 days a year that you will be using it. Find the drawbacks in what might be a gorgeous, ultra-streamlined motorhome or trailer that might later turn out to be uncomfortable or impractical for long-term use.

The Final Decision

Listen to all suggestions and reasons other people give you for getting certain sizes, floorplans, options, styles, etc., but make the final decision yourselves. Make that decision *alone (the couple),* without salespeople, Uncle Mortimer, and good buddy Henry. Their personal preferences are not necessary for your final decision.

I doubt if you will find the "perfect rig." All seem to have some drawbacks along with their many great features. I've always maintained that every decision in choosing an RV is a compromise. You give up one advantage to get another. For example, we would like a washer and dryer, but won't give up the space that we feel is important for other things. You have to choose between length and maneuverability, power and operating costs, tow and drive, and so on. If one opts for a large rig that gives ample space and comfort, then you must accept limitations on where you use it, less pulling power, and higher operating costs. Conversely, little rigs are wonderful for getting around, cost less, and are less expensive to operate, but are usually less comfortable, have less storage space, and fewer "bells and whistles." Speaking of the latter, it's wonderful to have every gadget made, but they all cost money. You get something, you give something.

Choosing the Right Type of RV

Of the five types—motorhomes, travel trailers, fifth wheels, pickup campers, and folding trailers—only the first three are popular with fulltimers. As to which is best, I can only say that it is up to the individual. Good arguments pro and con on each are possible. However, for the benefit of readers who are undecided, I'll present a few points they might consider in choosing an RV type.

Travel Trailers

The travel trailer is still the most popular full-timing rig, in part simply because it is generally the least expensive. I say *generally* because if one chooses a higher-priced trailer ($40,000 plus) and gets a top-of-the-line pickup (at $25,000 plus), he or she is definitely playing in the big leagues. However, one can buy 30-foot and over, brand-new trailers in the $15,000 range. If you happen to have a truck or car capable of towing a large trailer, then you can get into a nice, new full-timing rig with a minimum cash outlay.

Another plus for trailers is that they offer variety in their floorplans—featuring choices such as a middle kitchen, front kitchen, rear bath, or center bath.

A basic minus for trailers is the setup time required for

leveling and unhitching. Also, obviously one has to ride in the tow rig, which is often a pickup. Going to the bathroom, eating, or taking a nap requires stopping and getting out to get in the coach. On a rainy or cold day, that can be inconvenient. On the other hand, getting out for a stretch regularly is a good idea.

Fifth Wheels

Fifth-wheel vehicles are becoming increasingly popular with fulltimers, primarily because of their roominess and diversity of floorplans. The slide-out feature that gives them more floor space is being used on models from about 30 feet up. Most of the largest (40 feet) have from one to three slide-outs, and some companies make them 17 feet long. Consequently, fifth wheels are much more comfortable than other types of RVs simply because of the space they offer.

Floorplans in "fivers" are the most varied of any RV type. Generally the bedroom is up front in the part that overhangs the truck bed, but not always. Presently some companies are putting living rooms or lounge areas up there. Kitchens and dining areas may be in the middle or in the rear. Another especially good feature of the fifth wheel is its stability on the road — much better than travel trailers.

On the minus side, fifth wheels definitely require riding in a pickup truck. And they are heavy, sometimes extremely so (up to 11,000 pounds). They're easier to set up than a travel trailer, but they still require quite a bit of doing. Like the travel trailer, you must get out of the truck to use the coach. They are more expensive than trailers, too, with prices ranging up to $80,000. Combine the cost of the fifth wheel with the cost of the truck required to tow it, and you can have a very hefty investment.

Motorhomes

Motorhomes offer the greatest variety in subtypes: Class As, Class Bs, Class Cs, micro-minis, and low profiles. Generally, fulltimers choose Class As because of the room they offer. Besides variety in basic styles, motorhomes offer the widest choices in features, options, quality, and prices. As for the latter, prices can range from about $25,000 up to well over $500,000.

Undoubtedly the greatest feature of motorhomes is you're always inside it, whether driving or using it as a home. You can enjoy many of its features as you travel — use the bathroom, eat, take a nap, move about. Even the driver who stops to use the bathroom has only to take a few steps *inside* the coach to do so. Frequently, while traveling, Margie fixes me a snack to eat or a soft drink to sip as I drive. When one stops, just pull into the RV space, punch a button and leveling jacks come down to stabilize the rig. Actually it is then ready to use. A special aspect of motorhomes is the number of wonderful options available that aren't generally installed on travel trailers or fifth wheels: leveling jacks and generators, for example. We love the "basement" feature for carrying all our stuff.

On the minus side, motorhomes usually cost more than pull units (but not necessarily). You can't get as much variety in floorplans either. Also, the operating cost of a motorhome generally exceeds those of the other types.

The wisest choice is determined partly by preference and partly by use. For example, if you wish to travel extensively, here today, gone tomorrow, you can't beat a motorhome. The ease of setup is a major factor if you have to go through that procedure every night. However, if your normal pattern is to move only a few times a year, ease of operation may not be an important factor at all. Floor space and livability may be the most important features — or cost. If you have a very limited amount of money to spend on a rig, then you need to think in terms of the price.

In short, I can't tell you what would be best for you. I can only advise that you picture carefully how you expect to use the rig, think carefully how a potential choice that you are considering fits that picture, and make your own conclusion as to what is best for you.

And bear this in mind: The bad news is that the odds you will choose "the perfect rig" are about the same as those for winning the lottery. The good news is that no matter what your choice is, if you follow the "think directions" I've given you, you'll probably get along just fine with the vehicle you choose.

Chapter 20
Picking Up Extra Bucks

Most fulltimers are retired. That means no more punching a time clock five days a week. It also means no more paydays on Friday!

As a rule, those who have opted for a life on the road have regular incomes, in most cases Social Security, which is supplemented with company pensions or personal savings. However, it isn't uncommon for fulltimers to want or need to pick up extra dollars as they travel. Fortunately, there are many employment niches into which they can fit themselves.

Assuming that you are looking for only a part-time job or business, let's look at some areas for you to explore and some examples of how others have succeeded.

Market an Artistic Talent

Many retirees have talents that can be put to work. That work can be valuable in two ways: It provides an outlet for doing something interesting, and it might produce a marketable product.

You may recall that in Chapter 3, I referred to a woman who, although new at painting, has developed a talent to the point that she now sells her works. I met a metal sculptor in New Hampshire a few years ago who was working at a campground park table making beautiful brass creations that he sold at mall arts and crafts shows for amounts ranging up to $500. He towed a 24-foot trailer behind his van. The trailer was his home; the van was filled with raw materials and welding equipment.

Quartzite, Arizona, is the granddaddy of rock market

places. Rockhounds from all over the country congregate there every year to trade and sell the bounty of what are, in most cases, their hobbies.

I've seen some very fine woodcarvings offered for sale at flea markets and arts and crafts shows. Most are done by the sellers who turned their hobbies into sources of extra bucks. I once met a fellow at an Arizona flea market who displayed beautiful ironwood birds that he had learned to make after he retired.

Less talented artistically, perhaps, but certainly blessed in inventiveness, are those who turn simple, almost toally cost-free gadget- or trinket-manufacturing hobbies into money-making enterprises. I think particularly of a fellow I met in Florida last year who was parked just across the campground road from us. He worked at his camp table under his awning, turning beer cans into cute little airplanes with whirring propellers. He got ten dollars apiece for them and usually sold out quickly.

A couple we met several years ago had a stand at a flea market where each winter they sold their hobby specialties: in her case, beautiful and unique handmade sunbonnets; in his, wind chimes that he made from conduit. (They informed me confidentially that their hobby netted them $10,000 a year!) They worked and lived in a large travel trailer.

Anyone who has been to a flea market, especially the large ones, knows that almost anything can be sold. I would emphasize here, however, that it takes a particular temperament and personality to be involved regularly in this particular kind of marketing.

Last year I met an RVer at a show who was an itinerant clown. His converted bus contains not only living quarters for the couple but a barn for animals in the rear. His feature act is a goat that blows up balloons. He offers his services to RV shows and fairs.

Musically talented snowbirds are in great demand in the large snowbird roosts. Nearly every large park holds dances, so small bands that play "the oldies" can easily work two or three nights a week. (Twenty dollars a gig won't make anyone rich, but picking up an extra $200 or so each month while having fun isn't something to complain about.)

My list of examples could go on for pages, but there wouldn't be any point in that. Suffice it to say that many talents are marketable. Look around you at what others are doing and see how you can put your abilities to income-producing work.

Sell a Product

I've run across several enterprising fulltimers who were in effect simply "in business." A couple we met last year had a route that they serviced by selling packages of almonds. By purchasing the almonds in quantity at wholesale prices and repackaging them in small plastic bags, they created a product that sold well as snack food in service stations and other small retail outlets. Of course, they traveled in their home as they covered their route.

I've met several people who are dealers for some of the large door-to-door sales companies, such as Amway and Mary Kay Cosmetics.

One very popular way of making extra dollars, but which requires some investment, is to obtain and learn to use a machine that makes a product popular with RVers, such as name tags or personal license-plate holders. Or as one friend of mine has done, invent a gadget that will be popular with RVers. My friend made a telescoping metal handle with numerous attachments for cleaning RVs. Fulltimers with such products may attend as many RV shows as they wish and combine their business with visiting with other RVers.

Get a Job

Of course, there are innumerable opportunities to simply work at temporary jobs. I've met many RVers who work in campgrounds. Nearly every park hires extra help during the busy season, and what better source of good, knowledgeable workers than their RV customers? Many types of jobs are available, usually in maintenance (lawn mowing, cleaning, painting, or plumbing), or in the office.

For those who like real camping, the U.S. Forest Service

"host" program offers free space in exchange for hosting duties. Recently I discovered that some of the state parks also offer this deal. Besides the host program, there are many opportunities for paying jobs at concessions in national parks.

People with special skills or trades can frequently find temporary work when they want it. We met a couple last year who are affiliated with a company that takes inventory for various businesses. The couple simply sign up with the branch agencies that are in most cities and work when they want to. The distaff side of a couple parked across from us in the park we are in now has a computer and does special tax recording for small businesses they solicit wherever they are.

There's no end to the types of jobs one can get on a part-time basis as an RVer, but I'd like to end the subject with a report on two of the most interesting and unusual money-making methods I've come across.

The first was a fellow we met a dozen years ago in the Florida Keys, where he regularly spent his winters. He loved to fish, and he kept a nice boat at a marina near the park where he stayed. He really knew his stuff when it came to fishing, and every nice day (as most days were), he went out and returned with a good catch, which he sold to residents of the park or to the wholesaler at the dock! Some days he took in several hundred dollars. How's that for mixing business with pleasure?

The other case involved an attractive young woman who had her motorhome parked at a rest stop on I-8 between Yuma and Gila Bend in southern Arizona. Her *modus operandi* was to beam smiles at men without female companions, invite them in for coffee, tell a tale of woe, and in apparent desperation, offer her "personal attentions" for "gas money" to get her back to her home several states away. (Don't ask me how I know about this case, and I'm certainly not recommending it!)

In short, opportunities for fulltimers to trade know-how or muscle power for extra cash are almost unlimited. Add a little job-hunting effort, and you'll probably find a nice niche for yourself.

For information on campground work opportunities, inquire at individual national-forest or state-park offices. Also a publication that specializes in campground job information is *Workamper News*, 201 Hiram Road, HCR 34, Box 125, Heber Springs, Arkansas 72543.

Chapter 21
Fulltiming Isn't Forever

Making the decision to become a fulltimer can be very difficult. The prospect of giving up one's home, family, familiar
people, places, things, and the comfortable routines most of us
develop is indeed sobering. It should be—as any major change
in a family's way of doing things should be. I'm among the first
and loudest to recommend great care in making the decision.
But I'm equally quick to point out that a decision to take up
fulltiming isn't an ironclad, lifetime contract. Contrary to that
oft-stated claim that "you can't go home again," I reply, "Not
only can you go home again, most fulltimers at some point in
their lives do plant roots again."

Why RVers Give Up Fulltiming

Fulltimers return to "normal" living for many reasons.
Unfortunately, as they get older, ill health is often the
determining factor. Or just plain old age and the deterioration
of the human body demands a more settled life, one close to
particular doctors or health-care facilities. Sometimes
advancing age or ill health brings with it the need to be close to
family, especially children. Advancing age doesn't necessarily
mean the end of RVing. I'm aware of several instances in
which the "old folks" moved into parks near a child or even on
land owned by one of their children and still lived basically
independent lives in their own RVs.

Even if our health doesn't give out on us, eventually
Mother Nature (or the law) tells us that we can't handle our
big rigs properly or safely, and we have to give them up. I just
hope I'm smart enough to recognize that time and do it of my

own accord. Surely most of us will recognize the problem when we find ourselves having difficulties in making the fast and correct decisions that have to be made as pilots of big RVs. (Actually, *I* don't have to worry about making the decision — *Margie will make it for me!*)

Although many fulltimers are more or less forced to stop living on the road because of physical problems or old age, others give it up simply because they want to. Some discover marvelous places where the temptation to stay indefinitely is irresistible; others simply tire of being on the go and living in limited spaces. In short, most fulltimers have nothing to keep them from giving up that lifestyle any time they want to.

Another Option: Park Models

Several of my former full-timing friends have roots again but still retain many of the benefits and attributes of their former lifestyle. They have purchased spaces in condo or co-op RV parks, or they lease them on an annual basis. Many have purchased park-model trailers that provide some of the features of small houses — especially floor space and large appliances. Not uncommonly, they add patio rooms (also called Florida or Arizona rooms) that increase floor space to as much as 800 square feet, as much as many 1930s and 1940s houses.

The special attraction of living in park-model RV parks is that for RVers it's a way of eating one's cake and having it, too. If you're the kind who wants RV friends and the RV-park atmosphere, but with the kind of amenities that aren't offered in campgrounds or overnight parks, such as ballrooms, arts and crafts facilities, exercise programs, and lots of organized group activities, plus relatively large, comfortable quarters, you can get it by living in a snowbird park geared to this way of life. It also offers the advantage of being near to health-care facilities and where family members can both communicate or be with you as they wish.

Many park-model owners keep their motorhomes or trailers, which they have available for travels any time the mood strikes them. When they tire of being at home, they simply lock the doors of their park trailers; leave them within the security of walls, attended gates, and nearby neighbors; and head into the sunset.

Incidentally, one may wonder how wealthy you have to be to support all this. You might be surprised at how modestly priced some condo or co-op parks and park models are. Actually, park models are the least expensive per square foot of floor space of any RV (they're called RVs although they're more like small mobile homes).

A point that I'd like to emphasize here is that although park models are much like small mobile homes, they are used in RV parks, whereas mobile homes are used only in mobile-home parks. There's a considerable difference in lifestyles in the two kinds of parks. RV park people are generally more active, more outdoor oriented than mobile-home dwellers. They retain some of the carefree spirit of their traveling days, while most mobile-home dwellers lead more sedate, inside-oriented lives.

The cost of park-model spaces and park-model trailers can be just about any figure imaginable. Some nice lots can be purchased for under $10,000 and others may range up to as much as $100,000. It all depends on the kinds of amenities provided. For example, all condo developments have common facilities (those owned by all homeowners jointly). Most are quite nice, but within ordinary standards, while some have elegant structures and facilities, golf courses, even airstrips that make individual lot prices very high indeed.

Although I have talked with many semi-settled former fulltimers who have opted for owning or leasing permanent fixed quarters again, none expressed a desire to go back to exactly what they had before they took up fulltiming. They don't want their old home and all that went with it. Their general preferences now are for small, easy-to-maintain homes, such as condos or townhouses in resort areas they particularly liked when they were RVing. A few have even gone back to conventional houses, although rarely to their old stomping grounds.

The point is, if you're holding off from fulltiming because you aren't sure you want to spend the rest of your life living that way, bear in mind that you can go home again any time. However, that return may not be without financial loss, particularly if there is an attempt to duplicate what was given up. In some areas, real estate prices have escalated dramatically, making houses comparable to those sold several years ago unaffordable for some returnees to "regular" life. Also, it is unlikely the fulltiming rig can be sold for its purchase price.

On the other hand, giving up fulltiming can be an excellent opportunity to readjust to housing needs that are now different from those previously required. It could be an opportune time to choose a new locale, perhaps in the Sun Belt or in an area where living costs are relatively low. Empty nesters, as most fulltimers are, might opt for smaller quarters, such as condos or mobile homes.

In short, giving up fulltiming, although not without the potential for economic loss, generally presents more positive factors than negative.

Chapter 22
Making the Big Decision

The decision to go fulltiming is one of life's big ones. Only in a few other instances will the average person have the opportunity to choose a new direction for his or her life that will have the impact this one does. I have several suggestions that you might bear in mind when you are making this choice.

Make the Decision Together

First, and most important, it is absolutely crucial the decision be made jointly by both husband and wife (assuming you are a couple) and that you are both in agreement. I can't imagine anything more horrible than for a couple to sell their home, give up most of their possessions, leave their kids and grandkids, and take up a nomadic life if one of the parties is totally against the idea. I'm aware that, in many cases, one or both persons may have some misgivings about the change, but there's an enormous difference between "some misgivings" and "totally against." Most people who get into the full-timing lifestyle have some concerns about the future, but, like the sensible people they are, they weigh the pros and cons and generally come up with the right decision.

Set a Time

However, there are some people who never seem to be able to make up their minds. They think about fulltiming, they talk about it to anyone and everyone who will listen, they write to "experts" for advice, they talk to RV dealers, and some must dream about it—everything but make up their minds! I suspect some of them talk the years away and go to their eternal reward never having decided anything.

My suggestion is that anyone who is seriously contemplating life on the RV road should set a definite time to have their minds made up — six months, a year, whatever — and at the end of that time *either go or quit thinking and talking about it.*

Always bear in mind as you're working on a decision: If you choose to go, you'll probably be embarking on a way of life that will bring you all the joys you expected. However, if you try it and discover later that it isn't for you, you simply re-establish a fixed home again. But if you never make a decision at all, and instead keep thinking about it, you'll go through your retirement years always wondering what you missed.

The "Maxwell Fulltiming Aptitude Test"

Right now, do yourself a favor and take the "Maxwell Fulltiming Aptitude Test," found in Appendix I. It won't tell you positively what you should do, but it can indicate the direction you are leaning toward.

If it and/or the information on these pages have in any way helped you make up your mind about becoming a fulltimer, then I have succeeded in my goal.

I hope we'll meet on the road somewhere. If so, I'd like to shake your hand and hear your story.

Appendix I
The Maxwell Fulltiming Aptitude Test

The following questions pertain to your attitudes about how you want to live your life. The objective of the test is to compare your attitudes with those most characteristic of RV fulltimers in order to determine whether or not you are suited to the RV full-timing lifestyle. Choose the answers that *best* describe your feelings. If you would like someone else to take the test, write your responses on a separate sheet of paper. For scoring, see page 75.

Circle the answer that *best* describes your feelings.

1. Most of the time, I feel that
   a. I am happy and completely content with my home, family, and my present mode of living.
   b. I would like to *go* more, *do more,* and *see* more.
   c. we live in a lousy world, and there's not much anyone can do about it.

2. My idea of a perfect Sunday afternoon is
   a. to sit in a comfortable chair, eat snacks, and watch a TV special.
   b. to work at my hobby alone.
   c. to take a drive in the country on a road we've never taken before.

3. At a large gathering of people
   a. I sometimes start conversatons with strangers.
   b. I find a quiet spot at the side and watch.
   c. I talk only with people I know.

4. When planning a trip, I like to
   a. choose roads I am familiar with.
   b. select roads I've never taken before.
   c. stay on the interstates when possible.

5. My spouse
   a. is my best friend.
   b. bores me much of the time.
   c. generally does what he or she likes, and I do my own thing.

6. In heavy traffic or on mountain roads,
   a. I am usually nervous or terrified.
   b. I watch the scenery or the people in their cars.
   c. I am usually bored.

7. When something breaks around the house or won't work
   a. I usually try to fix it and frequently succeed.
   b. I usually just let it stay broken.
   c. I always call an expert to come and fix it.

8. My favorite book is
   a. a romance novel.
   b. an atlas.
   c. a spy thriller.

9. I enjoy most visiting
   a. shopping malls.
   b. historical houses.
   c. flea markets.

10. Given the choice, I would choose first to see
    a. Carlsbad Caverns.
    b. my favorite soap opera.
    c. a pro football game.

11. My favorite food is
    a. at restaurants.
    b. what I (or my spouse) prepares.
    c. what anyone else prepares.

12. My idea of the perfect way to travel is
    a. by air, staying and eating at hotels.
    b. by automobile, motels, and restaurants.
    c. by motorhome or travel trailer.

13. I would love to see more of
    a. Europe.
    b. Asia.
    c. the United States.

14. I am happiest when
    a. I am involved in a familiar routine.
    b. I am embarking on a new adventure.
    c. I am alone in my favorite room.

15. My experience in RVing:
    a. Never have done it so I don't know anything about it.
    b. Rather new at it but like it very much so far.
    c. Been at it for several years and love it.

16. How I feel about my home:
    a. It provides me with the roots that I must have.
    b. I love it, I am very sentimental about it, and could never give it up.
    c. I like it but it isn't absolutely crucial to my happiness.

17. How I feel about my kids and grandkids:
    a. I love them dearly but I have other things to do in life that cause me to be without them much of the time, and I can live with that.
    b. If I don't see them every few days, I am very, very unhappy.
    c. I feel that families should get together every Sunday and holiday.

18. Meeting new people is
    a. not very exciting or interesting.
    b. usually a pleasant experience and sometimes leads to new friends.
    c. a meaningless chore most of the time.

19. My preference in a vacation destination would be
    a. to visit relatives.
    b. Nova Scotia.
    c. a nice hotel in Chicago.

20. My spouse and I
    a. tolerate each other most of the time.
    b. often laugh at the same things.
    c. go along together without much fuss and feathers.

21. Given the option, I would usually
    a. drive 100 miles out of the way rather than drive through Los Angeles.
    b. drive over a curvy, mountain road rather than a flat desert road.
    c. not drive at all if I could ride with someone else.

22. Which of these would you be least likely to leave at home if you were taking a long trip in an automobile?
    a. Your tool box
    b. Your best suit
    c. Your favorite cassettes

23. Which would you *most* like to do?
    a. Spend a month at a Florida beach condo.
    b. Have a month in which to do absolutely no work or chores.
    c. Drive the Alaskan Highway.

24. Before I leave this earth, I would like most to
    a. visit all fifty states.
    b. save up a lot of money.
    c. be elected to a political office.

25. If I win the lottery, my first big purchase would be
    a. a new house.
    b. presents for all my relatives.
    c. a new motorhome or trailer.

Answers:

	13. c.
1. b.	14. b.
2. c.	15. c.
3. a.	16. c.
4. b.	17. a.
5. a.	18. b.
6. b.	19. b.
7. a.	20. b.
8. b.	21. b.
9. b.	22. a.
10. a.	23. c.
11. b.	24. a.
12. c.	25. c.

Scoring: Each correct answer counts one point.

23–25 — Your chances of becoming a successful fulltimer are excellent. Pack your rig and get going.

20–22 — Probably you will do okay, but you may have to work on a few problems now and then. Keep the house for a while.

15–19 — Success is up in the air. It looks like you would encounter some bumpy roads as a fulltimer. Test the waters carefully with a trial run (say six months) before you cut home ties.

10–14 — Success doubtful. If you try fulltiming, do so with your eyes open to the fact that you need to overcome some very anti-fulltiming attitudes.

9 or less — Do yourself (and others) a favor; you'll be happier if you stay at home.

Appendix II
Selecting an RV Home Base: State Tax & Registration Information

The facts and figures that follow were provided by the state agencies whose names and addresses appear at the end of each state's listing. As recommended in Chapter 4, "Choosing a Home Base," due to the fact of ever-changing state laws, you should contact those agencies before finalizing a state choice based on the information provided here. Up-to-date information may prove that laws have been changed.

State Tax & Registration Information

· Alabama ·

Financial Responsibilities
- State Income Tax: 2% for first $500, 4% for next $2500, 5% over $3000 for single filing. Rates same for marrieds filing jointly except income brackets are doubled
- State Sales Tax: 4% + optional city and county taxes

Vehicle Licensing and Registration
- Driver's License: $15 for 4 years
- Financial Responsibility: $20,000–$40,000 Public Liability; $10,000 Property Damage; not mandatory
- Vehicle Safety Inspection: No
- State Smog Device Required: No
- State Tax When Registering from Out of State: 2% user fee
- Title Transfer Fee: $15 + issuance fee
- Annual Vehicle Registration and Licensing: Registration—Passenger cars and pickups to 8000 lbs., $23. Pickups over 8000 and up to 12,000 lbs., $105. Truck and motorhome fees bases on gross weight to 8000 lbs., $23; 8000 to 12,000 lbs., $105. Motorcycles, $15. Tax—Based on 15% of fair value for private passenger vehicles

Voting
- Residency Requirements for Voter Registration: 1 day for federal elections; must register 10 days prior to election
- Address Requirements: Physical location
- Register by Mail: No

Additional Sources of Information
- Department of Revenue, P.O. Box 0001, Montgomery 36132-0001
- Alabama Department of Public Safety, PO Box 1551, Montgomery 36192

· Alaska ·

Financial Responsibilities
- State Income Tax: No
- State Sales Tax: Varies with each city and borough

Vehicle Licensing and Registration
- Driver's License: $10 for 5 years
- Financial Responsibility: $15,000–$20,000 Public Liability; $5000 Property Damage

- Vehicle Safety Inspection: No
- State Smog Device Required: Yes
- State Tax When Registering from Out of State: None
- Title Transfer Fee: $5
- Annual Vehicle Registration and Licensing: Registration — Passenger cars, $35. Pickups and vans, $40. Trailers, $5. Motorhomes, $35. Motorcycles, $20. Some counties charge registration tax, $60 1st year and declining

Voting
- Residency Requirements for Voter Registration: 30 days
- Address Requirements: Residence address
- Register by Mail: Yes

Additional Sources of Information
- Department of Revenue, State Office Building, P.O. Box SA, Juneau 99811
- Alaska State Troopers, 5700 E. Tudor Road, Anchorage 99507

· Arizona ·

Financial Responsibilities
- State Income Tax: Ranges from 2% to 8% with seven brackets, which are indexed annually for inflation
- State Sales Tax: 5% transaction privilege tax, 0.5% to 3% additions in some towns, cities and counties

Vehicle Licensing and Registration
- Driver's License: $7 for 4 years
- Financial Responsibility: $15,000–$30,000 Public Liability; $10,000 Property Damage. Mandatory insurance law
- Vehicle Safety Inspection: No
- State Smog Device Required: No
- State Tax When Registering from Out of State: None
- Title Transfer Fee: $4
- Annual Vehicle Registration and Licensing: Registration (vehicles may not be registered prior to entry) — All vehicles $8. Weight fee on ¾-ton and up trucks, 0-8000 lbs., $7.50; to 10,000 lbs., $36. Tax — Based on vehicle value, $4 per $100 of assessed value

Voting
- Residency Requirements for Voter Registration: 50 days
- Address Requirements: Physical address
- Register by Mail: No

Additional Sources of Information
- Department of Transportation, Motor Vehicle Division, 1801 W. Jefferson, Phoenix 85007
- Department of Revenue, 1600 W. Monroe, Phoenix 85007

· Arkansas ·

Financial Responsibilities
- State Income Tax: 1% to 7%, based on net taxable income
- State Sales Tax: 4%

Vehicle Licensing and Registration
- Driver's License: $13 for 4 years. Must visit office for photograph

- Financial Responsibility: $25,000–$50,000 Public Liability; $15,000 Property Damage
- Vehicle Safety Inspection: Yes, annually
- State Smog Device Required: No
- State Tax When Registering from Out of State: 3%, credit for prior tax paid
- Title Transfer Fee: $5
- Annual Vehicle Registration and Licensing: Registration (vehicles may be registered prior to entry) — Class 1 autos 3000 lbs. and less, $17; Class 2 autos 3001–4500 lbs., $24; Class 3 autos 4501 lbs. and over, $30; ½–¾-ton pickups, $21; motorhomes, $36. Trailers to 3000 lbs., $12 for 2 years; 3000 to 6000 lbs., $31 for 2 years; 6000 lbs. and up, $39 per year. Tax — Personal property tax on value of vehicle

Voting
- Residency Requirements for Voter Registration: No durational requirement; must register 20 days before election
- Address Requirements: Street address
- Register by Mail: No

Additional Sources of Information
- Arkansas Industrial Development Commission, One State Capitol Mall, Little Rock 72201
- Arkansas State Police, PO Box 5901, Little Rock 72215

• California •

Financial Responsibilities
- State Income Tax: 0% to 9.3%, depending on income
- State Sales Tax: 7.25%, some counties charge a total of up to 8.25%

Vehicle Licensing and Registration
- Driver's License: First time, $12 for 3 years; renewal, $12 for 4 years
- Financial Responsibility: $15,000-$30,000 Public Liability; $5,000 Property Damage. Required
- Vehicle Safety Inspection: No
- State Smog Device Required: Yes
- State Tax When Registering from Out of State: None if vehicle was purchased 90 days or before prior to bringing to state
- Title Transfer Fee: $9
- Annual Vehicle Registration and Licensing: Registration—All vehicles, $22 + $1 CHP fee. Tax—All vehicles, 2% of assessed value of vehicle

Voting
- Residency Requirements for Voter Registration: 29 days prior to election
- Address Requirements: Locational address
- Register by Mail: Yes

Additional Sources of Information
- Department of Motor Vehicles, Division of Registration, PO Box 932345, Sacramento 94232-3450
- Franchise Tax Board, Sacramento 95867

• Colorado •

Financial Responsibilities
- State Income Tax: 5% on modified federal taxable income (flat rate)
- State Sales Tax: 3% + local sales tax rate, if any

Vehicle Licensing and Registration
- Driver's License: $15 for 5 years
- Financial Responsibility: $25,000-$50,000 Public Liability; $15,000 Property Damage. Liability insurance compulsory
- Vehicle Safety Inspection: No
- State Smog Device Required: Yes
- State Tax When Registering from Out of State: None
- Title Transfer Fee: $1.50
- Annual Vehicle Registration and Licensing: Registration (vehicle must be physically present in Colorado prior to registration and titling) — Passenger vehicles including motorhomes 2000 lbs. and under, $6; 20¢ for each additional 100 lbs. up to 4500 lbs.; over 4500 lbs., $12.50; 60¢ for each additional 100 lbs. over 4500 lbs. Travel trailers 2000 lbs. or less, $4.50; over 2000 lbs., $9. Motorhomes over 6500 lbs., $24.50; 30¢ per 100 lbs. over 6500 lbs. Motorcycles, $3. Tax—Based on factory list price and vehicle year, minimum $3. First year 2.10% of taxable value to 9th year at .45%

Voting
- Residency Requirements for Voter Registration: 32 days
- Address Requirements: Street address
- Register by Mail: No

Additional Sources of Information
- Colorado State Patrol, Administrative Services Section, 700 Kipling, Suite 300, Lakewood 80215
- Department of Revenue, 1375 Sherman Street, Room 486, Denver 80203

• Connecticut •

Financial Responsibilities
- State Income Tax: Basic 4.5%
- State Sales Tax: 6%

Vehicle Licensing and Registration
- Driver's License: Exam fee, $29. License, $31 for 4 years
- Financial Responsibility: $20,000-$40,000 Public Liability; $5,000 Property Damage
- Vehicle Safety Inspection: Yes
- State Smog Device Required: No; annual emission test is required
- State Tax When Registering from Out of State: None
- Title Transfer Fee: $20 for title, $10 for transfer
- Annual Vehicle Registration and Licensing: Registration (vehicles may be registered prior to entry) — Passenger vehicles, $62 for 2 years; motorhomes and campers, $62 for 2 years. Trailers towed on a hitch, $16 for 2 years. Motorcycles, $30 for 2 years. Tax—Personal property based on value

Voting
- Residency Requirements for Voter Registration: No durational requirement; must register 21 days before a general election, 14 days before a primary
- Address Requirements: Street address
- Register by Mail: No

Additional Sources of Information
- Department of Motor Vehicles, Registry/Title Division, 60 State Street, Wethersfield 06109
- Department of Revenue Services, 92 Farmington Avenue, Hartford 06105

· Delaware ·

Financial Responsibilities
- State Income Tax: Progressive rate from 0.0% to 7.7% with 8 brackets
- State Sales Tax: None

Vehicle Licensing and Registration
- Driver's License: $12.50 for 5 years
- Financial Responsibility: $15,000–$30,000 Public Liability; $10,000 Property Damage
- Vehicle Safety Inspection: Yes, annually
- State Smog Device Required: No
- State Tax When Registering from Out of State: Vehicle Document Fee, 2% of fair market value
- Title Transfer Fee: $4
- Annual Vehicle Registration and Licensing: Registration—Passenger cars, $20. Trucks according to weight. Motorhomes and trailers, $2 for each 500 lbs. to 5000 lbs.; $2.60 for each 500 lbs. over 5000. Motorcycles, $10

Voting
- Residency Requirements for Voter Registration: No durational requirement; must register by third Sunday in October before a general election and 21 days before a primary
- Address Requirements: Post office box acceptable
- Register by Mail: Yes

Additional Sources of Information
- Department of Finance, Division of Revenue, Carvel State Office Building, 820 N. French Street, Wilmington 19801
- Department of Public Safety, Motor Vehicle Division, PO Box 698, Dover 19903

· District of Columbia ·

Financial Responsibilities
- State Income Tax: 6% for first $10,000 to $1400 plus 9.5% over $20,000
- State Sales Tax: 6%; 8% restaurant meals

Vehicle Licensing and Registration
- Driver's License: $15 for 4 years
- Financial Responsibility: Compulsory liability insurance required
- Vehicle Safety Inspection: Yes, annually
- State Smog Device Required: Yes
- State Tax When Registering from Out of State: 6% for vehicle under 3499 lbs.; over 3500 lbs., 7% of fair market value
- Title Transfer Fee: $10
- Annual Vehicle Registration and Licensing: Registration (vehicles may be registered prior to entry)—Passenger cars and motorhomes under 3499 lbs., $50; over 3500 lbs., $83. Trucks and trailers based on shipping weight, beginning at $25

Voting
- Residency Requirements for Voter Registration: 30 days
- Address Requirements: Residence address
- Register by Mail: Yes

Additional Sources of Information
- Bureau of Motor Vehicle Services, 301 C Street NW, Washington, D.C. 20001
- Department of Finance and Revenue, 300 Indiana Avenue NW, Room 4136, Washington, D.C. 20001

• Florida •

Financial Responsibilities
- State Income Tax. No
- State Sales Tax: 6% statewide; additional 1% local option taxes and tourist development taxes imposed in certain counties

Vehicle Licensing and Registration
- Driver's License: $15 for 6 years. Renew in person for 6 years or by mail for 4 years, $19
- Financial Responsibility: $10,000–$20,000 Public Liability
- Vehicle Safety Inspection: No
- State Smog Device Required: No. Emission testing in certain counties beginning in 1990
- State Tax When Registering from Out of State: 5%, less tax paid in another state
- Title Transfer Fee: $5
- Annual Vehicle Registration and Licensing: Registration (vehicle may be registered prior to entry) — Automobiles through 2499 lbs., $14.50; 2500–3499 lbs., $22.50; 3500 lbs. and over, $32.50. Private trucks through 1999 lbs., $14.50; 2000–3000 lbs., $22.50; 3001–5000 lbs., $32.50; 5001-5999 lbs., $45; 6000-7999 lbs., $65; 8000-9999 lbs., $76; 10,000-14,999 lbs.,$87. Travel trailers and fifth-wheels up to 35 ft., $20; over 35 ft., $25. Camping trailers, $10. Motorhomes less than 4500 lbs., $20; 4500 lbs. and over, $35. Motorcycles, $10. Mopeds and motorized bikes, $5

Voting
- Residency Requirements for Voter Registration: No durational requirement; must register 30 days before election
- Address Requirements: Physical address
- Register by Mail: No

Additional Sources of Information
- Department of Highway Safety and Motor Vehicles, Neil Kirkmen Building, Tallahassee 32301
- Department of Revenue, Carlton Building, Tallahassee 32301

• Georgia •

Financial Responsibilities
- State Income Tax: Gradual percentage with maximum of 6%
- State Sales Tax: 4% + 2% in Fulton County and 1% DeKalb County

Vehicle Licensing and Registration
- Driver's License: $4.50 for 4 years
- Financial Responsibility: No-fault insurance required
- Vehicle Safety Inspection: No
- State Smog Device Required: No
- State Tax When Registering from Out of State: None
- Title Transfer Fee: $5
- Annual Vehicle Registration and Licensing: Registration (vehicles may be registered prior to entry; must be registered within 30 days after moving into state) — Passenger cars, motorhomes and trailers, $8 + ad valorem tax based on retail value and millage rate of applicable county. Trucks based on gross weight. Motorcycles, $8. Tax — County ad valorem

Voting
- Residency Requirements for Voter Registration: No durational requirements; must register 30 days before election
- Address Requirements: Post office box acceptable
- Register by Mail: No

Additional Sources of Information
- Business Council of Georgia, 233 Peachtree St. NE, Atlanta 30303
- Department of Revenue, Motor Vehicle Unit, 126 Trinity Washington Building, Atlanta 30334

· Hawaii ·

Financial Responsibilities
- State Income Tax: 2¼% to 10% of taxable income
- State Sales Tax: 4% general excise tax

Vehicle Licensing and Registration
- Driver's License: $8.50 for 4 years between ages 25 and 64 years; $5.50 for 2 years for those under 25 and 65 and over
- Financial Responsibility: $25,000 Public Liability; $10,000 Property Damage. Must have Hawaii no-fault insurance
- Vehicle Safety Inspection: Yes, annually.
- State Smog Device Required: No
- State Tax When Registering from Out of State: None
- Title Transfer Fee: $3
- Annual Vehicle Registration and Licensing: Registration (state) — $10. Tax (county and city) — Passenger-carrying motor vehicles (private), ¾¢ per lb.; $12 minimum fee. Trucks and trailers, 1.5¢ per lb. (minimum 800 lbs., $12 tax on trailers). State tax .045¢ per lb. on vehicles under 6000 lbs. Motorcycles, minimum tax of $12

Voting
- Residency Requirements for Voter Registration: No durational requirement; must register 30 days before election
- Address Requirements: Verified street address
- Register by Mail: No

Additional Sources of Information
- Department of Taxation, PO Box 259, Honolulu 96809
- Division of Motor Vehicles and Licensing, City and County of Honolulu, 1455 South Beretania St., Honolulu 96814

· Idaho ·

Financial Responsibilities
- State Income Tax: 2% to 8.2%
- State Sales Tax: 5%, 2% on campground rates for 28 days or less

Vehicle Licensing and Registration
- Driver's License: $13.50 for 3 years
- Financial Responsibility: $25,000–$50,000 Public Liability; $15,000 Property Damage
- Vehicle Safety Inspection: No
- State Smog Device Required: Ada County only
- State Tax When Registering from Out of State: None with proof of ownership for 90 days or more
- Title Transfer Fee: $3
- Annual Vehicle Registration and Licensing: Registration (vehicles may be registered prior to entry) — Automobiles and motorhomes under 8000 lbs. 1–2 yrs. old, $36.48; 3–4 yrs. old, $33.48; 5–6 yrs. old, $26.28; 7–8 yrs. old, $22.68; over 8 yrs. old, $16.08. Travel trailers, $4. Trucks and motorhomes 80001-16,000 lbs., $31.08; 16,001-26,000 lbs., $61.08: 26,001-30,000 lbs., $91.68; 30,001-40,000 lbs., $130.08. Motorcycles $6.48. Annual RV sticker tax $5 per thousand of market value, plus $3.50

Voting
- Residency Requirements for Voter Registration: 30 days
- Address Requirements: Physical location
- Register by Mail: No

Additional Sources of Information
- Department of Transportation, Motor Vehicle Bureau, PO Box 7129, Boise 83707–1129
- State Tax Commission, 700 W. State Street, Boise 83720

· Illinois ·

Financial Responsibilities
- State Income Tax: 2½% individual, based on federal/AGI
- State Sales Tax: 6.25%, but local taxes apply; total rate varies from 6.25% to 8%

Vehicle Licensing and Registration
- Driver's License: $10 for 4 years; $5 for 69 years old or older; $5 for any duplicate or corrected license
- Financial Responsibility: $20,000–$40,000 Public Liability; $15,000 Property Damage
- Vehicle Safety Inspection: No
- State Smog Device Required: No
- State Tax When Registering from Out of State: None
- Title Transfer Fee: $3
- Annual Vehicle Registration and Licensing: Registration (vehicles may be registered prior to entry) — Passenger cars, $48. Truck fees based on weight. Recreational vehicles 8000 lbs. or less, $48; 8001 to 10,000 lbs., $60; 10,001 lbs. and over, $72. Recreational trailers 3000 lbs. and less, $12; 3001 to 8000 lbs., $22; 8001 to 10,000 lbs., $30; 10,001 lbs. and over, $40

Voting
- Residency Requirements for Voter Registration: 30 days
- Address Requirements: Street address
- Register by Mail: No

Additional Sources of Information
- Department of Revenue, 6th Level, SW Lower, 101 W. Jefferson Street, Springfield 62708
- Secretary of State, Motor Vehicle Division, Centennial Building, Springfield 62756

• Indiana •

Financial Responsibilities
- State Income Tax: 3%
- State Sales Tax: 5%

Vehicle Licensing and Registration
- Driver's License: $6 for 4 years
- Financial Responsibility: $25,000–$50,000 Public Liability; $10,000 Property Damage
- Vehicle Safety Inspection: No
- State Smog Device Required: No
- State Tax When Registering from Out of State: 5%. If vehicle was previously titled and registered in another state, no tax would be assessed
- Title Transfer Fee: $5
- Annual Vehicle Registration and Licensing: Registration — Passenger cars, $12.75. Motorhomes, $20.75. Trucks, travel trailers 3000 lbs. or less, $7.75; 3000 to 5000 lbs., $16.75; 5000 to 7000 lbs., $22.75. Motorcycles, $12.75. Tax — Determined by age and value, minimum $12

Voting
- Residency Requirements for Voter Registration: 30 days
- Address Requirements: Residency address
- Register by Mail: No

Additional Sources of Information
- Bureau of Motor Vehicles, Indiana State Office Building, 100 N. Senate Avenue, Indianapolis 46204

• Iowa •

Financial Responsibilities
- State Income Tax: Progressive rates of .40% to 9.98% for nine income brackets
- State Sales Tax: 4%

Vehicle Licensing and Registration
- Driver's License: $8 for 2 years; $16 for 4 years
- Financial Responsibility: $20,000–$40,000 Public Liability; $15,000 Property Damage
- Vehicle Safety Inspection: No
- State Smog Device Required: No
- State Tax When Registering from Out of State: None if 4% tax paid at original purchase
- Title Transfer Fee: $10

- Annual Vehicle Registration and Licensing: Registration—Passenger cars 40¢ per 100 lbs. + 1% of list price. After fifth year and through ninth year, fee is reduced. Tenth year value is 10%. Travel trailers 20¢ per square foot of floor space through 6 years, 15¢ thereafter. Motorhomes—Class A with value of $20,000 or less 1–5 years old, $120, $85 thereafter; $20,000–$39,999 1–5 years old, $140, $105 thereafter; $40,000–$79,999 1–5 years old, $200, $150 thereafter; $80,000 and over, $400, $300 thereafter. Class B 1–5 years, $90; $65 thereafter. Class C 1–5 years, $110; $80 thereafter. Motorcycles, $20; after 5 years, $10

Voting
- Residency Requirements for Voter Registration: No durational requirement; must register 10 days before election
- Address Requirements: Post office box acceptable if street address does not exist
- Register by Mail: Yes

Additional Sources of Information
- Information and Management Services Division, Iowa Department of Revenue, Hoover State Office Building, Des Moines 50319
- Motor Vehicle Division, Vehicle Registration, Iowa Department of Transportation, Lucas State Building, Des Moines 50319

• Kansas •

Financial Responsibilities
- State Income Tax: Individuals pay 4.8% of Kansas taxable income for $27,500 or less and $1320 plus 6.1% of excess over $27,500; married individuals filing joint returns pay 4.05% of Kansas taxable income for $35,000 or less and $1418 plus 5.3% of excess over $35,000
- State Sales Tax: 4%; cities and counties can levy up to an additional 1%

Vehicle Licensing and Registration
- Driver's License: Class C (passenger vehicles and RVs), $8; Motorcycles, $5 + $1. Photo fee, $1; exam fee, $3
- Financial Responsibility: $25,000–$50,000 Public Liability; $10,000 Property Damage
- Vehicle Safety Inspection: No
- State Smog Device Required: No
- State Tax When Registering from Out of State: 4% of value
- Title Transfer Fee: $9 until Jan. 1, 1990; $3.50 thereafter
- Annual Vehicle Registration and Licensing: Registration (vehicles may be registered prior to entry) — Passenger vehicles and motorhomes 3000 lbs. or less, $13; 3000–4000 lbs., $16.25; 4000–4500 lbs., $19.50; over 4500 lbs., $26. Travel trailers 8000 lbs. or less, $10; 8000–12,000 lbs., $15; over 12,000 lbs., $25. Motorcycles, $10

Voting
- Residency Requirements for Voter Registration: 20 days
- Address Requirements: Specific address or location
- Register by Mail: Yes

Additional Sources of Information
- Division of Vehicles, State Office Building, Topeka 66626
- Department of Revenue, 2nd Floor, State Office Building, Topeka 66612

• Kentucky •

Financial Responsibilities
- State Income Tax: 2% on first $3000 of net income to 6% on excess of $8000
- State Sales Tax: 5%

Vehicle Licensing and Registration
- Driver's License: $8 for 4 years, $2 for duplicate. Motorcycles, $3 for 4 years. Renew by mail
- Financial Responsibility: $25,000–$50,000 Public Liability; $10,000 Property Damage
- Vehicle Safety Inspection: No
- State Smog Device Required: No, except Jefferson County
- State Tax When Registering from Out of State: 5% of value. Credit allowed with all states, must have tax receipts
- Title Transfer Fee: $6 base
- Annual Vehicle Registration and Licensing: Registration—Passenger cars, $14. Motorhomes, $21. Travel trailers less than 25 ft., $5.50; over 25 ft., $10.50. Trucks based on weight, i.e. 6000 lb. gross, $13.50. Motorcycles, $6. Tax—Personal property

Voting
- Residency Requirements for Voter Registration: 30 days
- Address Requirements: Street address
- Register by Mail: Yes

Additional Sources of Information
- Department of Transportation, Motor Vehicle Division, State Office Building, Frankfort 40622
- Revenue Cabinet, Commonwealth of Kentucky, Frankfort 40620

• Louisiana •

Financial Responsibilities
- State Income Tax: 2% for first $10,000, 4% on next $40,000 and 6% on excess over $50,000 for individuals; double income brackets for joint filing
- State Sales Tax: 4% + local options in some parishes

Vehicle Licensing and Registration
- Driver's License: $18 for 5 years
- Financial Responsibility: $10,000–$20,000 Public Liability; $10,000 Property Damage
- Vehicle Safety Inspection: Yes, annually
- State Smog Device Required: Yes, on 1980 models and up
- State Tax When Registering from Out of State: The same as other states require of Louisiana residents
- Title Transfer Fee: $18.50
- Annual Vehicle Registration and Licensing: Registration—Private passenger cars, $12 for 4 years. Motorhomes, $25 yearly. Travel trailers, $10 yearly. Vans and trucks under 3500 lbs., $40 for 4 years. Motorcycles, $12 for 4 years. Tax—On first registration only

Voting
- Residency Requirements for Voter Registration: No durational requirement; must register 24 days before a general election, 30 days before a primary

- Address Requirements: Street address
- Register by Mail: No

Additional Sources of Information
- Department of Revenue and Taxation, PO Box 201, Baton Rouge 70821
- Louisiana State Police, Research Unit, PO Box 66614, Baton Rouge 70896

• Maine •

Financial Responsibilities
- State Income Tax: 2% to 8.5% of Maine adjusted gross income; for nonresident individuals, only that part of federal adjusted gross income derived from sources within Maine is subject to the tax
- State Sales Tax: 6%; 7% on rentals charged for tourist or trailer camps

Vehicle Licensing and Registration
- Driver's License: $20 for 4 years
- Financial Responsibility: $20,000-$40,000 Public Liability; $10,000 Property Damage
- Vehicle Safety Inspection: Annually
- State Smog Device Required: No
- State Tax When Registering from Out of State: 5%, credit given for prior tax paid
- Title Transfer Fee: $10
- Annual Vehicle Registration and Licensing: Registration (vehicles may be registered prior to entry. A municipal excise tax based on value payable upon registration) — Passenger cars, $22. Trailers up to 2000 lbs., $8.50; in excess of 2000 lbs., truck rate. Motorhomes, farm fee rates. Motorcycles, $18; mopeds, $6

Voting
- Residency Requirements for Voter Registration: No durational requirement; may register on election day
- Address Requirements: Street address
- Register by Mail: Yes

Additional Sources of Information
- Deputy Secretary of State, Division of Public Services, Motor Vehicle Division, Augusta 04333
- Bureau of Taxation, State Office Building, Augusta 04333

• Maryland •

Financial Responsibilities
- State Income Tax: 2% on taxable net income of $1000 and under; $20 + 3% of excess over $1000 for income over $1000 to $2000; $50 + 4% of excess over $2000 for income over $2000 to $3000; $90 + 5% of excess over $3000 for income over $3000
- State Sales Tax: 5%

Vehicle Licensing and Registration
- Driver's License: Original, $22 for 4 years. Renewal, $6 for 4 years. Renew in person
- Financial Responsibility: $20,000-$40,000 Public Liability; $10,000 Property Damage

- Vehicle Safety Inspection: Yes, on used vehicles
- State Smog Device Required: No
- State Tax When Registering from Out of State: 5%, credit is given for prior tax paid when registering within 30 days of moving to state
- Title Transfer Fee: New vehicles, $1; used vehicles, $3
- Annual Vehicle Registration and Licensing: Registration (vehicles may be registered prior to entry) — Passenger cars and motorhomes up to 3700 lbs., $27; over 3700 lbs., $40.50. Travel trailers to 3000 lbs., $10; 3000–5000 lbs., $27; to 10,000 lbs., $47.25. Trucks, weight fee. Motorcycles, $10.50

Voting
- Residency Requirements for Voter Registration: 29 days
- Address Requirements: Street address; post office box acceptable if that particular post office does not deliver mail
- Register by Mail: Yes

Additional Sources of Information
- Comptroller of the Treasury, PO Box 466, Annapolis 21404-0466
- Department of Transportation, 6601 Richie Highway NE, Room 120, Glenn Burnie 21062

· Massachusetts ·

Financial Responsibilities
- State Income Tax: 5.95% tax on earned income and Massachusetts bank interest; 12% tax on other interest and divided income; 6% effective tax rate on capital gains income. Residents pay tax on all income regardless of source. Non-residents pay taxes on income earned in Massachusetts only
- State Sales Tax: 5%

Vehicle Licensing and Registration
- Driver's License: $43.50 for 5 years; $20 additional charge for out-of-state applicants; $15 exam fee
- Financial Responsibility: $15,000-$20,000 Public Liability; $5,000 Property Damage
- Vehicle Safety Inspection: Yes, annually
- State Smog Device Required: No
- State Tax When Registering from Out of State: 5% sales tax + excise tax of $25 per $1,000 of valuation; credit allowed for prior tax paid
- Title Transfer Fee: $50
- Annual Vehicle Registration and Licensing: Registration (vehicles may be registered prior to entry) — Automobiles, $45 for 2 years. Auto homes, $35 for 1 year with camper plates. Trailers, $12 per 1000 lbs. When renewing registrations by mail, there is a $5 discount

Voting
- Residency Requirements for Voter Registration: No durational requirement; must register 28 days before election
- Address Requirements: Street address
- Register by Mail: No

Additional Sources of Information
- Department of Revenue, Executive Office for Administration and Finance, 100 Cambridge Street, Room 806, Boston 02202
- Registry of Motor Vehicles, Customer Assistance Bureau, 100 Nashua Street, Boston 02114

• Michigan •

Financial Responsibilities
- State Income Tax: 4.6%
- State Sales Tax: 4%

Vehicle Licensing and Registration
- Driver's License: $12 for 4 years; renewal $12 for 4 years
- Financial Responsibility: No-fault insurance required
- Vehicle Safety Inspection: No
- State Smog Device Required: No, but emission test certificate may be required to register in Detroit Metro area
- State Tax When Registering from Out of State: 4% use tax on value if not registered and paid to another state
- Title Transfer Fee: $10
- Annual Vehicle Registration and Licensing: Registration—Passenger vehicles, pickup trucks and motorhomes, 1984 or later model year, based on manufacturer's suggested base price. $0–$6,000, $30; more than $6000–$7000, $33; more than $7000–$8000, $38; more than $8000–$9000, $43; more than $9000–$10,000, $48; more than $10,000–$11,000 $53; more than $11,000–$12,000, $58; more than $12,000–$13,000, $63; more than $13,000–$14,000, $68; more than $14,000–$15,000, $73; more than $15,000–$16,000, $78; more than $16,000–$17,000, $83; more than $17,000–$18,000, $88; more than $18,000–$19,000, $93; more than $19,000–$20,000, $98; more than $20,000–$21,000, $103; more than $21,000–$22,000, $108; more than $22,000–$23,000, $113; more than $23,000–$24,000, $118; more than $24,000–$25,000, $123; more than $25,000–$26,000, $128; more than $26,000–$27,000, $133; more than $27,000–$28,000, $138; more than $28,000–$29,000, $143; more than $29,000–$30,000, $148; more than $30,000, 0.5% of the list price. Vehicle registration fee for 1983 and older models based on weight of vehicle. Trailer coaches based on weight from 251 lbs to 505 lbs are $7 to $46; 5051 lbs and over are 76¢ per 100 pounds plus $5. Motorcycles, $23. Tax—Ad valorem fee based on vehicle's value

Voting
- Residency Requirements for Voter Registration: 30 days
- Address Requirements: Street address
- Register by Mail: No

Additional Sources of Information
- Compliance and Rules Division, Department of State, Mutual Building, 208 N. Capitol Avenue, Lansing 48918
- Bureau of Collections, Department of Treasury, Treasury Building, Lansing 48909

• Minnesota •

Financial Responsibilities
- State Income Tax: 6% to 8% with brackets determined by filer type; 0.5% surtax on certain higher incomes
- State Sales Tax: 6%; an additional 2½% on on-sale and off-sale liquor

Vehicle Licensing and Registration
- Driver's License: $10 for 4 years; Class A, $30; Class B, $22.50; Class C, $15
- Financial Responsibility: No-fault insurance required

- Vehicle Safety Inspection: Random spot inspection
- State Smog Device Required: No
- State Tax When Registering from Out of State: 6%, credit allowed for prior tax paid
- Title Transfer Fee: $6 + $3.25 filing fee
- Annual Vehicle Registration and Licensing: Registration (vehicles may be registered prior to entry) — Automobiles, ad valorem tax, $10 + 1.25% of vehicle base value, minimum $35. Recreational vehicles according to gross weight. Motorcycles, $10; mopeds, $6

Voting
- Residency Requirements for Voter Registration: 20 days immediately preceding election
- Address Requirements: Physical address
- Register by Mail: Yes

Additional Sources of Information
- Department of Public Safety, Driver and Vehicle Services Division, State Transportation Building, St. Paul 55155
- Department of Revenue, Tax Research Division, Mail Station 2230, 10 River Park Plaza, St. Paul 55146-2230

· Mississippi ·

Financial Responsibilities
- State Income Tax: 3% on first $5000; 4% on next $5000, 5% over $10,000
- State Sales Tax: 6%

Vehicle Licensing and Registration
- Driver's License: $13 for 4 years
- Financial Responsibility: $10,000–$20,000 Public Liability; $5000 Property Damage
- Vehicle Safety Inspection: Yes, annually
- State Smog Device Required: No
- State Tax When Registering from Out of State: Nonapplicable
- Title Transfer Fee: $5
- Annual Vehicle Registration and Licensing: Registration — Base fee, $10. Tax — Ad valorem tax in county of residence + bridge privilege tax. Passenger cars, $15. Trailers, $10. Tax reduced each year after model year until 50%. Motorcycles, $8

Voting
- Residency Requirements for Voter Registration: 30 days
- Address Requirements: Street address
- Register by Mail: No

Additional Sources of Information
- Director of Government Services, Mississippi Economic Council, 656 N. State Street, PO Box 1849, Jackson 39215-1849
- State Tax Commission, Privilege Tax Division, PO Box 1140, Jackson 39205

· Missouri ·

Financial Responsibilities
- State Income Tax: 1½% to 6%, depending on taxable income; 6% maximum rate at $9000
- State Sales Tax: 4.225% + various local taxes

Vehicle Licensing and Registration
- Driver's License: $7.50 for 3 years (Class 1 operator)
- Financial Responsibility: Security-type law is applicable in event of accident causing property damage to any one person in excess of $500 or personal injury or death; no judgment minimum. Minimum financial responsibility limit: $25,000/$50,000/$10,000
- Vehicle Safety Inspection: Yes, annually, $4.50
- State Smog Device Required: No
- State Tax When Registering from Out of State: 4.225% sale or use
- Title Transfer Fee: $7.50
- Annual Vehicle Registration and Licensing: Registration (vehicles may be registered prior to entry) — Automobiles, 1–11 hp, $18; 12–23 hp, $21; 24–35 hp, $24; 36–47 hp, $33; 48–59 hp, $39; 60–71 hp, $45; 72 hp and over, $51. Trucks 6000 lbs. and under, $25.50, 6001–12,000 lbs., $38. Recreational vehicles, $32. Trailers, $7.50. Motorcycles, $8.50; motor tricycles, $10

Voting
- Residency Requirements for Voter Registration: No durational requirement; must register 20 days before election
- Address Requirements: Street address
- Register by Mail: Yes

Additional Sources of Information
- Department of Revenue, Motor Vehicle Bureau, Box 100, Jefferson City 65102
- Department of Revenue, Truman Building, PO Box 629, Jefferson City 65105
- Secretary of State's Office, Box 778, Jefferson City 65101

· Montana ·

Financial Responsibilities
- State Income Tax: 2% on taxable income of $1,300 and less to 11% minus $1,645 on taxable income over $57,000 (10 brackets)
- State Sales Tax: None

Vehicle Licensing and Registration
- Driver's License: $16 for 4 years
- Financial Responsibility: $25,000-$50,000 Public Liability; $5,000 Property Damage
- Vehicle Safety Inspection: No
- State Smog Device Required: No
- State Tax When Registering from Out of State: None on models over 1 year old
- Title Transfer Fee: $3
- Annual Vehicle Registration and Licensing: Registration (vehicles may be registered prior to entry) — Automobiles and light trucks less than 4 years old 2850 lbs. or under, $70; over 2850 lbs., $90. Vehicles more than 4 years, less than 8, 2850 lbs. or under, $40; over 2850 lbs., $50. Vehicles 8 years and older, 2850 lbs. or under, $10; over 2850 lbs., $15. Motorhomes less than 2 years old, $200, to 8 years and older at $15. House trailers (park model), $2.50 plus 75¢ per foot. Motorized house cars and trucks, $10.50 plus weight fee. Motorcycles depend on number of ccs and age, $4—$80

Voting
- Residency Requirements for Voter Registration: 30 days
- Address Requirements: Physical residence
- Register by Mail: Yes

Additional Sources of Information
- Department of Revenue, Mitchell Building, Helena 59620
- Registrar Bureau, Motor Vehicle Division, 925 Main Street, Deer Lodge 59722

• Nebraska •

Financial Responsibilities
- State Income Tax: 2.37% to 6.92% of taxable income with four brackets
- State Sales Tax: 5%. Additional increase subject to change; some municipalities have city sales taxes

Vehicle Licensing and Registration
- Driver's License: $10 for 4 years
- Financial Responsibility: $25,000–$50,000 Public Liability; $25,000 Property Damage
- Vehicle Safety Inspection: No
- State Smog Device Required: No
- State Tax When Registering from Out of State: None
- Title Transfer Fee: $6
- Annual Vehicle Registration and Licensing: Registration (vehicles may be registered prior to entry) — Passenger cars, $15. Motorized house cars, travel trailers based on gross weight. Motorhomes 8000 lbs. or less, $18; 8001–11,999 lbs., $30; 12,000 lbs. or over, $42. Trucks based on gross weight plus load. Motorcycles, $4.50

Voting
- Residency Requirements for Voter Registration: No durational requirement; must register 10 days before election
- Address Requirements: Street address or voting precinct or ward
- Register by Mail: No

Additional Sources of Information
- Department of Motor Vehicles, Box 94789, Lincoln 68509-4789
- Department of Revenue, Box 94818, Lincoln 68509-4818

• Nevada •

Financial Responsibilities
- State Income Tax: None
- State Sales Tax: 6.5% to 7% depending on county

Vehicle Licensing and Registration
- Driver's License: $20.50 for 4 years
- Financial Responsibility: $15,000-$30,000 Public Liability; $10,000 Property Damage
- Vehicle Safety Inspection: No
- State Smog Device Required: Clark and Washoe counties; other counties have option to require device

- State Tax When Registering from Out of State: 5.75% out-of-state purchase; 3.75% purchase from individual; .25% higher in counties and city listed above
- Title Fee: $10
- Annual Vehicle Registration and Licensing: Registration—Passenger cars, buses, motorized house cars, travel trailers, $33. All others according to weight. Additional fees based on year, make and model. Motorcycles, $17. Tax—Priviledge tax, $4 per $100 valuation on depreciated value

Voting
- Residency Requirements for Voter Registration: 30 days
- Address Requirements: Physical address
- Register by Mail: No; registration can be done at Department of Motor Vehicles facilities

Additional Sources of Information
- Department of Motor Vehicles, Registration Division, 555 Wright Way, Carson City 89711
- Department of Taxation, 1340 S. Curry Street, Carson City 89710

• New Hampshire •

Financial Responsibilities
- State Income Tax: 5% on some investment income
- State Sales Tax: None; 8% meals and rooms tax

Vehicle Licensing and Registration
- Driver's License: $30 for 4 years
- Financial Responsibility: $20,000–$50,000 Public Liability; $5000 Property Damage. Not required
- Vehicle Safety Inspection: Yes, annually, during month of registered owner's birthday
- State Smog Device Required: No
- State Tax When Registering from Out of State: Based on value, but not less than $2
- Title Transfer Fee: $5
- Annual Vehicle Registration and Licensing: Registration (vehicles may be registered prior to entry)—Pleasure-type cars up to 3000 lbs., $19.20; 3001–5000 lbs., $31.20; 5001–8000 lbs., $43.20; 8001 and over, 84¢ per 100 lbs. Travel trailers, trucks based on weight. Tax—Based on value of vehicle, minimum $2

Voting
- Residency Requirements for Voter Registration: 10 days
- Address Requirements: Physical address
- Register by Mail: No

Additional Sources of Information
- Division of Motor Vehicles, Hayes Safety Building, 10 Hazen Dr., Concord 03305
- Department of Revenue Administration, PO Box 467, Concord 03301

▪ New Jersey ▪

Financial Responsibilities
- State Income Tax: 2% of taxable income not over $20,000; $400 + 2.5% of excess over $20,000 for taxable income over $20,000 but not over $50,000; $1150 + 3.5% of excess over $50,000 for taxable income over $50,000
- State Sales Tax: 7%

Vehicle Licensing and Registration
- Driver's License: $8 for 2 years; motorcycles $4 for 2 years. Renew by mail
- Financial Responsibility: $15,000–$30,000 Public Liability; $5000 Property Damage
- Vehicle Safety Inspection: Yes, annually
- State Smog Device Required: Yes
- State Tax When Registering from Out of State: None, if taxes are currently paid in previous state
- Title Transfer Fee: $4; $5 with lien on vehicle
- Annual Vehicle Registration and Licensing: Registration (vehicles may be registered prior to entry) — Manufactured prior to 1971 less than 2700 lbs. shipping weight, $14; 2700–3800 lbs., $23; in excess of 3800 lbs., $44. Manufactured 1971 through 1979 less than 2700 lbs. shipping weight, $17; 2700–3800 lbs., $28; in excess of 3800 lbs., $51. Manufactured 1980 or thereafter, no greater than 3500 lbs. shipping weight, $25; in excess of 3500 lbs., $50. Private utility and house-type trailers or semitrailers, $4 for less than 2000 lbs. gross weight; $9 for 2000 lbs. and over. Motorcycles, $10. Add $2.50 inspection fee to all above

Voting
- Residency Requirements for Voter Registration: 30 days
- Address Requirements: Street address
- Register by Mail: Yes

Additional Sources of Information
- Division of Motor Vehicles, 25 S. Montgomery Street, Trenton 08666
- Department of Treasury, Division of Taxation, 50 Barrack Street, CN-269, Trenton 08646

▪ New Mexico ▪

Financial Responsibilities
- State Income Tax: 1.8% to 8.5% for singles filing; 2.4% to 8.5% for spouses filing jointly and heads of households
- State Sales Tax: 4.75% + local options

Vehicle Licensing and Registration
- Driver's License: $10 for 4 years. $2.50 per year for motorcycle
- Financial Responsibility: $25,000–$50,000 Public Liability; $10,000 Property Damage
- Vehicle Safety Inspection: No
- State Smog Device Required: No, except for Albuquerque
- State Tax When Registering from Out of State: 3% of value, credit for prior tax paid
- Title Transfer Fee: $5.30

- Annual Vehicle Registration and Licensing: Registration (vehicles may be registered prior to entry) — Passenger vehicles registered 5 years or less up to 2000 lbs., $20; 2001–3000 lbs., $29; over 3001 lbs., $42. Vehicles registered over 5 years up to 2000 lbs., $16; 2001–3000 lbs., $23; 3001 lbs. and over, $34. House trailers, $5. Trucks based on gross weight and year. Motorcycles, $11

Voting
- Residency Requirements for Voter Registration: No durational requirement; must register 42 days before election
- Address Requirements: Physical address
- Register by Mail: No

Additional Sources of Information
- Department of Taxation and Revenue, PO Box 630, Santa Fe 87509
- Transportation Department, Division of Motor Vehicles, 1100 S. St. Francis Drive, Santa Fe 87503

· New York ·

Financial Responsibilities
- State Income Tax: 4% to 7.875% with five brackets
- State Sales Tax: 4%, except for the 12 counties from Dutchess County south to New York City where the state sales tax is 4.25% (.25% imposed for benefit of the Metropolitan Commuter Transportation District)

Vehicle Licensing and Registration
- Driver's License: $16 for 4 years + $1.50 photo fee
- Financial Responsibility: $50,000–$100,000 Death Liability; $10,000–$20,000 Injury Liability; $5000 (minimum) Property Damage
- Vehicle Safety Inspection: Yes, annually
- State Smog Device Required: Yes
- State Tax When Registering from Out of State: 4% + any local tax (if applicable)
- Title Transfer Fee: $2.50 (pending legislation change)
- Annual Vehicle Registration and Licensing: Registration — Passenger cars and motorhomes, 75¢ per 100 lbs. up to 3500 lbs. $1.12½ per 100 lbs. over 3500 lbs., minimum $15. House trailers, $1.20 per 100 lbs. (unladen weight), minimum $15. Trucks, $2.50 per each 500 lbs. gross weight. Motorcycles, $10

Voting
- Residency Requirements for Voter Registration: 30 days
- Address Requirements: Physical address
- Register by Mail: Yes

Additional Sources of Information
- Department of Motor Vehicles, Empire State Plaza, Albany 12228
- Department of Taxation and Finance, W.A. Harriman State Office Building Campus, Albany 12227

· North Carolina ·

Financial Responsibilities
- State Income Tax: 6% to 7.75%
- State Sales Tax: 4% + 2% local levies in all counties

Vehicle Licensing and Registration
- Driver's License: $10 for 4 years. Renew by mail
- Financial Responsibility: $25,000–$50,000 Public Liability; $10,000 Property Damage
- Vehicle Safety Inspection: Yes, annually
- State Smog Device Required: Yes
- State Tax When Registering from Out of State: 2% of value, not to exceed $300. Credit for prior tax paid
- Title Transfer Fee: $5
- Annual Vehicle Registration and Licensing: Registration (vehicles may be registered prior to entry) — Private passenger vehicles, $20. Motorhomes, $20. Travel trailers, $10. Motorcycles, $9. Tax — Personal property tax by cities and counties

Voting
- Residency Requirements for Voter Registration: 30 days
- Address Requirements: Street address
- Register by Mail: No

Additional Sources of Information
- Division of Motor Vehicles, 1100 New Bern, Raleigh 27697
- Department of Revenue, 2 S. Salisbury Street, Raleigh 27611

• North Dakota •

Financial Responsibilities
- State Income Tax: 14% of federal income tax liability (simplified optional method)
- State Sales Tax: 5%

Vehicle Licensing and Registration
- Driver's License: $10 for 4 years
- Financial Responsibility: $25,000–$50,000 Public Liability; $25,000 Property Damage
- Vehicle Safety Inspection: None
- State Smog Device Required: No
- State Tax When Registering from Out of State: 5½%, credit for prior tax paid
- Title Transfer Fee: $5
- Annual Vehicle Registration and Licensing: Registration (vehicles may be registered prior to entry) — Passenger motor vehicles based on weight and year model. Travel trailers, $20. Motorcycles, $21

Voting
- Residency Requirements for Voter Registration: 30 days
- Address Requirements: Physical location
- Register by Mail: No voter registration

Additional Sources of Information
- Tax Department, 8th Floor, State Capitol, Bismarck 58505
- Motor Vehicle Department, Capitol Grounds, Bismarck 58505

· Ohio ·

Financial Responsibilities
- State Income Tax: 0.808% of Ohio taxable income $5000 and less to $5006.75 + 8.075% of excess over $100,000 for incomes over $100,000
- State Sales Tax: 5%; additional county or transit taxes can apply

Vehicle Licensing and Registration
- Driver's License: $5 for 4 years + $1.50 issuance fee; duplicate $1.50; lamination (if desired) $1; vision screening on subsequent renewal $1
- Financial Responsibility: $12,500–$25,000 Public Liability; $7500 Property Damage
- Vehicle Safety Inspection: Yes, random
- State Smog Device Required: No
- State Tax When Registering from Out of State: 5% credit given for prior tax paid
- Title Transfer Fee: $2
- Annual Vehicle Registration and Licensing: Passenger cars, $20; motorhomes and noncommercial trucks, $35. No refund on unexpired plates. Issuance fee $1.50, reflectorizing 50¢, county identification sticker upon acquiring new plates or changing county of residence 25¢ per set. Trucks based on net weight; travel trailers, $10

Voting
- Residency Requirements for Voter Registration: Reside in state 30 days per year
- Address Requirements: Street address
- Register by Mail: Yes

Additional Sources of Information
- Driver and Vehicle Services, State Highway Patrol, Box 7037, Station E, Columbus 43266–0562
- Department of Taxation, PO Box 530, Columbus 43266

· Oklahoma ·

Financial Responsibilities
- State Income Tax: 0% to 6% without federal tax deduction; 0% to 17% with federal tax deduction
- State Sales Tax: 4.5% + applicable local tax

Vehicle Licensing and Registration
- Driver's License: $20 for 4 years
- Financial Responsibility: $10,000-$20,000 Public Liability; $10,000 Property Damage
- Vehicle Safety Inspection: Yes
- State Smog Device Required: No
- State Tax When Registering from Out of State: Registration fee due upon establishing residency; no credit for prior registration taxes paid. Excise tax due unless owned and registered in former state of residence at least 60 days prior to registering in Oklahoma; excise tax based on original total delivered price and age of vehicle
- Title Transfer Fee: $11
- Annual Vehicle Registration and Licensing: New vehicle—$15 road use fee + $2.75 administrative fee + 1.25% of the factory-delivered price; 2nd through 12th year fee—90% of the previous year's factory delivered price

+ road use fee + administrative fee; 13th through 20th year fee = the 12th year fee; 21 years and older—annual fee $18.

Voting
- Residency Requirements for Voter Registration: No durational requirement; must register 10 days before election
- Address Requirements: Street address
- Register by Mail: No

Additional Sources of Information
- Oklahoma Tax Commission, Motor Vehicle Division, 2501 Lincoln Blvd., Oklahoma City 73194
- Oklahoma Department of Public Safety, PO Box 11415, Oklahoma City 73136

• Oregon •

Financial Responsibilities
- State Income Tax: 5% to 9%, three brackets. 9% rate at $5000 taxable for single return, $10,000 for joint return
- State Sales Tax: None

Vehicle Licensing and Registration
- Driver's License: $25, valid for 3 to 5 years, depending on how near your birthday is when you apply and the year you were born
- Financial Responsibility: $25,000–$50,000 Public Liability; $10,000 Property Damage
- Vehicle Safety Inspection: No
- State Smog Device Required: No
- State Tax When Registering from Out of State: None
- Title Transfer Fee: $9
- Annual Vehicle Registration and Licensing: Registration (applicants are required to certify that they are domiciled in Oregon or otherwise eligible for Oregon registration)—Passenger cars, $20. Motorhomes, $56 + $3 per foot over 10 ft. Travel trailers, $36 + $3 per foot over 10 ft. Trucks based on weight. Motorcycles, $6. All fees for 2 years

Voting
- Residency Requirements for Voter Registration: 20 days
- Address Requirements: Street address
- Register by Mail: Yes

Additional Sources of Information
- Department of Transportation, Motor Vehicles Division, 1905 Lana Avenue NE, Salem 97314
- Department of Revenue, Revenue Building, 955 Center Street NE, Salem 97310

• Pennsylvania •

Financial Responsibilities
- State Income Tax: 2.1%
- State Sales Tax: 6%

Vehicle Licensing and Registration
- Driver's License: $20 for 4 years + $2 photo (one-time fee). Renew by mail

- Financial Responsibility: $15,000–$30,000 Public Liability; $5000 Property Damage
- Vehicle Safety Inspection: Yes, annually
- State Smog Device Required: No, except for certain areas
- State Tax When Registering from Out of State: 6%, exempt if more than 6 months old and out-of-state
- Title Transfer Fee: $4
- Annual Vehicle Registration and Licensing: Registration (vehicles may be registered prior to entry) — Passenger cars, $24 per year. Motorhomes 8000 lbs. or less, $30; 8001–11,000 lbs., $42; 11,001 lbs. and more, $54. Trailers 3000 lbs. or less, $6; 3001–10,000 lbs., $12; 10,000 lbs. and more, $27. Trucks 5000 lbs. or less, $39; 5001–7000 lbs., $54; 7001–9000 lbs., $102; 9001–11,000 lbs., $132. Retirees qualify for reduced fee of $10 for any one vehicle not weighing over 9000 lbs. regular gross weight. Motorcycles, $12

Voting
- Residency Requirements for Voter Registration: 30 days
- Address Requirements: Street address
- Register by Mail: Yes

Additional Sources of Information
- Department of Revenue, 1131 Strawberry Square, Harrisburg 17127
- Department of Transportation, Bureau of Motor Vehicles, Information Services Section, PO Box 8269, Harrisburg 17105

· Rhode Island ·

Financial Responsibilities
- State Income Tax: 27.5% of federal tax
- State Sales Tax: 6%

Vehicle Licensing and Registration
- Driver's License: $8 for 2 years, first time; $20 for 5 years renewal. New picture required every 5 years
- Financial Responsibility: $25,000-$50,000 Public Liability; $10,000 Property Damage. Insurance not required
- Vehicle Safety Inspection: Yes, annually
- State Smog Device Required: Yes
- State Tax When Registering from Out of State: 7%, credit for tax paid to another state
- Title Transfer Fee: $5
- Annual Vehicle Registration and Licensing: Registration (vehicles may be registered prior to entry) — Automobiles and motorhomes under 2500 lbs., $10; 2500-3000 lbs., $11; 3000-3500 lbs., $12; 3500-4000 lbs., $14; 4000-4500 lbs., $17; 4500-5000 lbs., $20; 5000-5500 lbs., $24; 5500-6000 lbs., $28; over 6000 lbs., $33. Travel trailers, pickup campers under 3000 lbs., $5; over 3000 lbs., 15¢ per 100 lbs. gross weight including load. Trucks based on gross weight. Motorcycles, $13

Voting
- Residency Requirements for Voter Registration: 90 days
- Address Requirements: Street address
- Register by Mail: No

Additional Sources of Information
- Division of Taxation, Department of Administration, 289 Promenade Street, Providence 02903
- Registry of Motor Vehicles, State Office Building, Providence 02903

· South Carolina ·

Financial Responsibilities
- State Income Tax: 3% to 7%
- State Sales Tax: 5% retail + 2% accommodations

Vehicle Licensing and Registration
- Driver's License: $10 for 4 years
- Financial Responsibility: $15,000–$30,000 Public Liability; $5000 Property Damage
- Vehicle Safety Inspection: Yes
- State Smog Device Required: No
- State Tax When Registering from Out of State: 5% or $300, whichever is less
- Title Transfer Fee: $5; license transfer fee, $3
- Annual Vehicle Registration and Licensing: Registration—Passenger cars and motorized houses, $13. Camp trailers to 30 ft., $6; over 30 ft., $7. Trucks based on weight. Motorcycles, $6. Tax—County and municipal personal property

Voting
- Residency Requirements for Voter Registration: No durational requirement; must register 30 days before election
- Address Requirements: Post office box or street address
- Register by Mail: No

Additional Sources of Information
- Tax Commission, PO Box 125, Columbia 29214
- Motor Vehicle Division, Department of Highways and Public Transportation, PO Box 1498, Columbia 29216

· South Dakota ·

Financial Responsibilities
- State Income Tax: None
- State Sales Tax: 4%

Vehicle Licensing and Registration
- Driver's License: $6 for 4 years
- Financial Responsibility: $25,000–$50,000 Public Liability; $25,000 Property Damage
- Vehicle Safety Inspection: No
- State Smog Device Required: No
- State Tax When Registering from Out of State: 3%
- Title Transfer Fee: $5
- Annual Vehicle Registration and Licensing: Registration (vehicles may be registered prior to entry)—Noncommercial motor vehicles 2000 lbs. or less, $20; 2001–4000 lbs., $30; 4001–6000 lbs., $40; 6001–7000 lbs., $60; 7001–8000 lbs., $80; 8001–9000 lbs., $100; 9001–10,000 lbs., $120;

10,001–11,000 lbs., $140; 11,001–12,000 lbs., $160; 12,001–13,000 lbs., $180; each additional 1000 lbs. or major fraction thereof, in excess of 13,000 lbs., $40. Recreational motor bus, $100. Noncommercial trailers 1000 lbs. or less, $5; 1001–2000 lbs., $15; 2001–3000 lbs., $25; 3001–4000 lbs, $35; 4001–5000 lbs., $45; 5001–6000 lbs., $55; 6001–7000 lbs., $65; 7001–8000 lbs., $75; 8001–9000 lbs., $85; 9001–10,000 lbs., $95; each additional 1000 lbs. or major fraction thereof, in excess of 10,000 lbs., $10. Motorcycles with piston displacement of less than 350 cubic centimeters, $7.50; 350 cubic centimeters or more, $10

Voting
- Residency Requirements for Voter Registration: No durational requirement; must register 15 days before election
- Address Requirements: Post office box is acceptable, but must be able to define a specific location
- Register by Mail: No

Additional Sources of Information
- Department of Motor Vehicles, 118 W. Capitol Avenue, Pierre 57501
- Department of Revenue, 3rd Floor, Kenip Building, Pierre 57501

• Tennessee •

Financial Responsibilities
- State Income Tax: 6% on limited items of interest and most dividends
- State Sales Tax: 5½% + 2¼% average local rate

Vehicle Licensing and Registration
- Driver's License: $16 operator for 4 years; $2 exam fee. Renew by mail; if over 65, renewal is $12
- Financial Responsibility: $20,000–$40,000 Public Liability; $10,000 Property Damage
- Vehicle Safety Inspection: No. County inspection fee (wheel tax) levied in some counties; rates vary from $10 to $50
- State Smog Device Required: No
- State Sales Tax When Registering Vehicle Purchased Out of State: 5½% + local tax
- Title Transfer Fee: $5
- Annual Vehicle Registration and Licensing: Registration (vehicles may be registered prior to entry) – Passenger cars, $20.50. Motorhomes by weight. Travel trailers, $11.25. Trucks, maximum gross weight. Motorcycles, $13.50

Voting
- Residency Requirements for Voter Registration: 50 days; must register 30 days prior to election
- Address Requirements: Street address
- Register by Mail: Yes

Additional Sources of Information
- Department of Revenue, 200 Andrew Jackson Building, Nashville 37242
- Highway Patrol, Department of Safety, 1150 Foster Avenue, Nashville 37210

· Texas ·

Financial Responsibilities
- State Income Tax: None
- State Sales Tax: 6%

Vehicle Licensing and Registration
- Driver's License: $16 for 4 years
- Financial Responsibility: $20,000–$40,000 Public Liability; $15,000 Property Damage
- Vehicle Safety Inspection: Yes
- State Smog Device Required: Yes
- State Tax When Registering from Out of State: $15 new-resident use tax
- Title Transfer Fee: $10 for new title, $2.50 for transfer
- Annual Vehicle Registration and Licensing: Registration (vehicles may be registered prior to entry) — Passenger cars and motorhomes more than 6 years from date of annual registration, $40.50; more than 3 years but 6 years or less from date of annual registration, $50.50; 3 years or less from date of annual registration, $58.50; any vehicle over 6000 lbs. irrespective of model year, $25 + 60¢ cwt. Travel trailers and trucks based on gross weight. Motorcycles, $30.75. $5 may be collected by county for each vehicle registered (not all counties collect this fee)

Voting
- Residency Requirements for Voter Registration: No durational requirement; must register 30 days before election
- Address Requirements: Street address
- Register by Mail: Yes

Additional Sources of Information
- Office of Comptroller of Public Accounts, Room 809, LBJ Building, Austin 78774
- Traffic Law Enforcement, Texas Department of Public Safety, Box 4087, Austin 78773

· Utah ·

Financial Responsibilities
- State Income Tax: 3¾% to 7¾% joint returns; 2¾% to 7¾% single returns
- State Sales Tax: 5^{27}/32% to 6¼%

Vehicle Licensing and Registration
- Driver's License: $10 for 4 years
- Financial Responsibility: $15,000–$30,000 Public Liability; $5000 Property Damage. Compulsory no-fault insurance required for all vehicles except trailers and motorcycles
- Vehicle Safety Inspection: Yes, annually
- State Smog Device Required: No
- State Tax When Registering from Out of State: 4¾%, credit allowed for tax paid to another state
- Title Transfer Fee: $2
- Annual Vehicle Registration and Licensing: Registration (vehicles may be registered prior to entry) — Passenger cars, $10; house trailers in excess of 750 lbs. unladen weight, $7.50; trucks based on gross weight, 6000 lbs., $12.50; 9000 lbs., $20; motorcycles, $7.50. $1 per plate reflectorization fee. Tax — County personal property

Voting
- Residency Requirements for Voter Registration: 30 Days
- Address Requirements: Street address
- Register by Mail: Yes

Additional Sources of Information
- Utah Highway Patrol, 4501 S. 2700 West, Salt Lake City 84119
- Tax Commission, Heber Wells Building, 160 E. 300 South, Salt Lake City 84134

▪ Vermont ▪

Financial Responsibilities
- State Income Tax: 25% of federal tax
- State Sales Tax: 4%

Vehicle Licensing and Registration
- Driver's License: $10 for 2 years, $16 for 4 years
- Financial Responsibility: $20,000–$40,000 Public Liability; $10,000 Property Damage. Mandatory
- Vehicle Safety Inspection: Yes, annually
- State Smog Device Required: No; must meet federal regulations
- State Tax When Registering from Out of State: 4% of value
- Title Transfer Fee: $5; $8 with lien
- Annual Vehicle Registration and Licensing: Registration (vehicles may be registered prior to entry)—Pleasure cars and motorhomes, $36. Trailer coaches with loads less than 1500 lbs., $8.45; over 1500 lbs., $16.90. Trucks to 6000 lbs., $36; 6000–8000 lbs., $9.70 per 1000 lbs. Motorcycles, $11.25; mopeds, $11.25

Voting
- Residency Requirements for Voter Registration: No durational requirement; must register 17 days before election
- Address Requirements: Physical location
- Register by Mail: No

Additional Sources of Information
- Motor Vehicle Hearing Unit, Department of Motor Vehicles, 120 State Street, Montpelier 05603–0001
- Department of Taxes, Agency of Administration, PO Box 694, Montpelier 05601-0694

▪ Virginia ▪

Financial Responsibilities
- State Income Tax: 2% of $3000 and under taxable income; $60 + 3% of $3000–$5000 taxable income; $120 + 5% of $5000–$12,000 taxable income; $470 + 5.75% of taxable income over $12,000
- State Sales Tax: 3% + 1% local tax

Vehicle Licensing and Registration
- Driver's License: $2.40 per year + $1 for any endorsements
- Financial Responsibility: $25,000–$50,000 Public Liability; $10,000 Property Damage
- Vehicle Safety Inspection: Yes, annually
- State Smog Device Required: Yes

- State Tax When Registering from Out of State: 2%, credit for prior tax paid
- Title Transfer Fee: $10
- Annual Vehicle Registration and Licensing: Registration (vehicles may be registered prior to entry) — Passenger cars 4000 lbs. and under, $22; over 4000 lbs., $27. Motorhomes 4000 lbs. and under, $22; over 4000 lbs., $27. Travel trailers, $7.50. Trucks 4000 lbs. and under, $22; 4001–6500 lbs., $27; 6501–7500 lbs., $33; 7501–10,000 lbs., $32

Voting
- Residency Requirements for Voter Registration: No durational requirement; must register 31 days before election
- Address Requirements: Street address
- Register by Mail: No

Additional Sources of Information
- Department of State Police, PO Box 27472, Richmond 23261-7472
- Department of Taxation, 2220 W. Broad Street, Richmond 23220

· Washington ·

Financial Responsibilities
- State Income Tax: None
- State Sales Tax: 7% to 8.1%

Vehicle Licensing and Registration
- Driver's License: $14 for 4 years, $7 exam fee. Renew by mail one time. Motorcycle endorsement $5
- Financial Responsibility: $25,000–$50,000 Public Liability; $10,000 Property Damage
- Vehicle Safety Inspection: No, except first time registered. $10 fee for out-of-state inspection
- State Smog Device Required: In certain areas only
- State Tax When Registering from Out of State: 7% to 8.1%, credit for prior sales or use tax paid
- Title Transfer Fee: $4, plus use tax if due
- Annual Vehicle Registration and Licensing: Registration — Passenger cars, motorcycles, $27.75 (renewal $23.85). Travel trailers, $28.75 (renewal $24.75). Campers, $5.90 (renewal $4.50). Motorhomes, $28.85 (renewal $24.85). Trucks license fee based on gross weight. Tax — 2.454% of market value

Voting
- Residency Requirements for Voter Registration: 30 days
- Address Requirements: Street address
- Register by Mail: No

Additional Sources of Information
- Department of Revenue, Taxpayer Information Section, General Administration Building, MS/AX-02, Olympia 98504
- Department of Licensing, Highways-Licenses Building, Olympia 98504

· West Virginia ·

Financial Responsibilities
- State Income Tax: 3% to 6.5%, depending on income
- State Sales Tax: 6%

Vehicle Licensing and Registration
- Driver's License: $10 for 4 years, renew by mail
- Financial Responsibility: $20,000/$40,000/$10,000 Public Liability; $10,000 Property Damage
- Vehicle Safety Inspection: Yes
- State Smog Device Required: Yes
- State Tax When Registering from Out of State: 5% of market value
- Title Transfer Fee: $5
- Annual Vehicle Registration and Licensing: Registration (vehicles may be registered prior to entry) — Passenger-type vehicles under 3000 lbs., $25; 3000–4000 lbs., $30; over 4000 lbs., $36. Trailers less than 2000 lbs., $8; campers, $12. Trucks by gross weight. Motorcycles, $8. 50¢ insurance recording fee. Tax — Personal property tax, $1 litter fee

Voting
- Residency Requirements for Voter Registration: 30 days
- Address Requirements: Street address
- Register by Mail: Yes

Additional Sources of Information
- State Tax Department, PO Drawer 2389, Charleston 25328
- Department of Motor Vehicles, 1800 Washington Street E, Charleston 25317

• Wisconsin •

Financial Responsibilities
- State Income Tax: Top rate of 7.9%, 4 tax brackets with a sliding scale standard deduction that varies with income
- State Sales Tax: 5% + applicable local tax, if any

Vehicle Licensing and Registration
- Driver's License: $9 + $5 road test if applicable, first time for 2 years. $9 for 4-year renewal
- Financial Responsibility: $25,000–$50,000 Public Liability; $10,000 Property Damage
- Vehicle Safety Inspection: No
- State Smog Device Required: Cannot remove any manufacturer-installed devices
- State Tax When Registering from Out of State: 5%, credit for prior tax paid
- Title Transfer Fee: $5
- Annual Vehicle Registration and Licensing: Registration (vehicles may be registered prior to entry) — Automobiles, $25. Mobile homes 25 ft. or under, $12; over 25 ft., $18. Trucks — 4500 lbs., $30; 6000 lbs., $42; 8000 lbs., $57; 1,200 lbs., $135. Motorhomes according to gross weight; 5000 lbs., $30, to 12,000 lbs., $48. Motorcycles, $7

Voting
- Residency Requirements for Voter Registration: 10 days prior to election
- Address Requirements: Street address
- Register by Mail: Yes

Additional Sources of Information
- Department of Revenue, Revenue Audit Bureau, PO Box 8906, Madison 53708
- Department of Transportation, Office of Public Affairs, PO Box 7910, Madison 53707

· Wyoming ·

Financial Responsibilities
- State Income Tax: None
- State Sales Tax: 3% + optional counties' levies

Vehicle Licensing and Registration
- Driver's License: $10 for 4 years
- Financial Responsibility: $25,000–$50,000 Public Liability; $20,000 Property Damage
- Vehicle Safety Inspection: No
- State Smog Device Required: No
- State Tax When Registering from Out of State: 4% to 5%, depending on county. Credit for prior tax paid
- Title Transfer Fee: $5 until 1/1/90, then $6
- Annual Vehicle Registration and Licensing: Registration (vehicle must be checked in Wyoming before title is issued) — Passenger cars, $15. Trailers, motorhomes, trucks based on unladen weight. Motorcycles, $5. Tax — County registration fee. First year 3% of 60% of factory price; second year 3% of 50%; third year 3% of 40%; fourth year 3% of 30%; fifth year 3% of 20%; sixth year 3% of 15%; and the same for each year thereafter, minimum fee $5

Voting
- Residency Requirements for Voter Registration: No durational requirement; must register 30 days before election
- Address Requirements: Street address
- Register by Mail: No

Additional Sources of Information
- State Tax Commission, Department of Revenue and Taxation, Herschler Building, Cheyenne 82002–0110